Atlantis

Atlantis

Lost Kingdom of the Andes

J.M. Allen

Floris Books

First published in 2009 by Floris Books
© J.M. Allen 2009

The publishers would like to thank the following for the use of extracts and illustrations:
The translated extracts from Plato and the grid plan of the Island of Atlantis, page 100 (Fig. 7.03) are reproduced by permission of the publishers and the Trustees of the Loeb Classical Library from PLATO: VOLUME IX, Loeb Classical Library ®, Volume 234, translated by R.G. Bury, pp. 29–43, 265–305, Harvard University Press, © 1929 The President and Fellows of Harvard College, Cambridge, Mass. USA. The Loeb Classical Library ® is a registered trademark of the President and Fellows of Harvard College.

An alternative translation used for comparison is that by Sir Desmond Lee, *Plato's Timaeus* and *Critias* in Penguin Classics, revised edition 1977, © 1965, 1971, 1977 H.D.P. Lee, by permission of Penguin Books, UK.

For further comparison, the translations of *Critias* and *Timaeus* by Sir Benjamin Jowett (1817–93) were also used, from Vol.3 of *The Dialogues of Plato,* Oxford University Press, 1892.

Photos, page 75 (Figs. 5.01 and 5.02) by arrangement with John Villegas, Zingara Travel, La Paz.
Illustration, page 80 (Fig. 6.02) by permission of Ron Miller.
Illustration, page 93 (Fig. 6.22) Lee Smart.
Illustration, page 124 (Fig. 10.05), René Rojas, La Paz, Bolivia.
Satellite images on pages 102–105 (Figs. 7.05–7.11, 14.02–14.05, B.18) courtesy of Digital Globe and Google Earth
Illustration page 162 (Fig. 12.15) courtesy of Time-Life Books

The publishers also wish to thank anyone whose photographs may have been used in this book and who may not have received proper acknowledgment if the source was unknown. Any such oversight will be corrected in future editions.

British Library CIP Data available

ISBN: 978-086315-697-7

Printed in Singapore

Contents

1. Introduction   11

2. The Great Secret of the Indias   41

3. The Tomb of the Incas   51

4. History and Legends of the Incas   61

5. The Aymara language and the *Fuente Magna*   73

6. Atlantis Today   79

7. Sinking into the Sea   95

8. The Circle and the Cross   107

9. Stones and Cactus   113

10. An Invitation to Oruro   121

11. Completing the Trail   135

12. From Tarija to Tiwanaku   145

13. The Dating Question   163

14. Postscript   167

Appendix A   177
Comparative table of locations/attributes needed for site of Atlantis,
based on Milos Atlantis Conference criteria, 2005

Appendix B   181
Fifty Point Comparison between Atlantis and the Altiplano

Appendix C   204
Greek Gods

Appendix D   205
Andean Gods

Atlantis at Pampa Aullagas: map   206

References and Sources   207

Acknowledgments

I would like to give a special thanks to Samuel Doria Medina and SOBOCE S.A. (Bolivia) for their support whilst writing this book.

Also I would like to express my appreciation and thanks to: Carlos and Anna Aliaga, Cochabamba; John Villegas and the Villegas family of Zingara Travel, La Paz; Ing Jorge Román, Hilka Tellez de Román of the Hotel Max Plaza, Oruro; Reynaldo Solis of GPS, Bolivia; Alfredo Villca; Aerosur.

'Para nosotros la patria es la América.' Simón Bolívar.

'South Americans shouldn't call themselves South Americans but rather Atlanteans.'
Jim Allen, interviewed by Carlos Quiroga, Reuters, October 1999.

1. Introduction

It is said that people like a mystery. And one of the greatest puzzles of modern times is the story of Atlantis, a great continent which the Greek philosopher Plato said sank into the sea in the space of a single day and night. To this day, no one has been able to say with any certainty where the location of Atlantis was, nor even whether it really existed.

Many suggestions have been put forward as a site for the lost continent. Atlantis, according to Plato himself, lay in the Atlantic Ocean, 'opposite the Pillars of Hercules' which the Greek geographer Strabo, writing around AD 17–23, tells us meant the Strait of Gibraltar, specifically the mountains of Calpe on the Gibraltar side and Abilyx, the mountain in Libya on the opposite side, though Strabo also tells us that others had the opinion that the pillars were actual pillars set up in the temple of Hercules on the island of Gades (modern Cadiz) or other locations nearby.

Certain modern writers in an attempt to justify the theory that Atlantis was on Thera and Crete have attempted to relocate the Pillars to within the eastern Mediterranean, but their efforts are pointless since whether the Pillars were located at Gibraltar or inside the Mediterranean, Plato specifically states that the Atlanteans had as their base the island of Atlantis which was 'at a distant point in the Atlantic Ocean'.

Atlantis was also 'larger than Libya and Asia combined' and had a whole host of other attributes none of which apply to Thera or Crete. Other popular locations such as the Azores, have never been part of a sunken continent and indeed modern geology tells us that it is impossible for a land mass the size of a continent to sink into the sea in the space of a single day and night as Plato claimed.

Even wildly improbable locations such as Antarctica have their adherents, even though Antarctica has never suffered 'earth crust displacement' as has been claimed, and in any event has been under ice for at least 100,000 to 200,000 years according to modern research, whereas Plato gave a date for Atlantis as nine thousand years before Solon, or say around 9600 BC if solar years were intended.

I agree with the words of a professor from Newcastle speaking on a radio interview where he said, 'if a site is to be considered as the site of Atlantis, then it must reasonably conform to the description of Atlantis as given by Plato'. The Atlantis Milos International Conference 2005 put forward a list of twenty-four attributes it considered appropriate for the location of Atlantis, and in Appendix A (see p. 177) we show how each proposed site 'scores' against Plato's description. It can be seen that, at the present time, not only do the majority of sites put forward as the location of Atlantis not conform to the geographic description given by Plato, they are frequently the opposite of his description.

Fig. 1.01. Model of the island continent with the rectangular level plain arrowed. The translation from Plato by Sir Desmond Lee tells us: '... in the centre of the island near the sea was a plain which was enclosed by mountains, and the region as a whole was high above the level of the sea ....' (And he adds the footnote, 'i.e. midway along its greatest length.') '... The plain was naturally a long, regular rectangle'. (Lee 1965)

And the fundamental question, of course, which haunts all researchers into the subject of Atlantis is the question of whether Plato made up the subject of Atlantis as part of his moral tale about the ideal city state, or whether it was based on an actual location or events.

Since the majority of archaeologists and professional philosophers follow the belief that Atlantis was entirely fictional, made up by Plato as part of his ideal city story, they also, in consequence reject outright any efforts to establish an actual location for the region that Plato described and it is quite usual for them not even to examine any such evidence as may be offered them, such is their adherence to the established viewpoint. Yet it may be said in their defence that so many locations have been offered as the site of Atlantis and so many distortions have been added to the original story of Atlantis (such as death-ray crystals and clairvoyant predictions), that the subject has been rendered outside the bounds of credibility.

Yet in Plato's story there is nothing more than an elaborate geographic description of the continent he called Atlantis and a description of how it engaged in a war with ancient Athens and Egypt, being defeated by the ancient city state of Athens. That, after all, was his stated purpose of his story — to find a worthy enemy with which his ancient city state could engage in war and show how his ancient Athens was 'the bravest in war and supremely well organized'.

So in his search for a suitable story to illustrate the military valour of ancient Athens, did he indeed use, as he claimed, a story brought back to Greece from Egypt by the Greek statesman Solon, or were all these numerous geographic details entirely invented?

The test must be this: is there a geographic location or sequence of events that matches the actual description given by Plato? My proposed solution is that the lost continent of Atlantis is still there opposite the Pillars of Hercules (Strait of Gibraltar) only now it has been re-named *South America*. Using the Atlantis Milos Conference list of twenty-four attributes considered appropriate for the location of Atlantis, already referred to above, we can readily establish that the Bolivian Altiplano conforms to at least twenty and has many more not listed by the conference. In fact, there are around fifty specific points from the Atlantis story which can be demonstrated to relate to the site in South America (see Appendix B on p. 181).

The key to the mystery of Atlantis is that Plato is describing both a large continent and a small volcanic island of the same name. The continent had a large, level rectangular plain at its centre and in the centre of the plain was the small volcanic island which became the city of Atlantis.

According to Plato, too, 'the whole region was high above the level of the sea, rising sheer out of the sea to a great height'. (*Critias,* 118A, Bury 1929) The Benjamin Jowett translation adds 'lofty and precipitous *on the side of the sea'.*

Yet, as we saw above, Plato also states that the city was on a level plain and only 5 miles (8 km) from the sea and connected to the sea by a canal. The only way the city can be on a level plain and 5 miles from the sea and yet at the same time 'high above the level of the sea' is if there are in fact *two* seas, that is, the *Ocean Sea* surrounding the island continent and the *inland sea* adjacent to the city.

Plato's description exactly fits South America because that is the continent which is opposite the Pillars of Hercules and because the level rectangular plain he wrote about is to be found in the centre of that continent, midway along the longest side exactly as he described it. The city in turn lay on this level rectangular plain, 50 stades (5 miles or 8 km) from the 'sea' which, in this context, has to be an *inland sea.* Therefore it was not the *continent* of Atlantis which sank into the sea, but the island capital of the same name, built around a volcanic island which sank into an inland sea. After my researches discovered the rectangular plain in the area now called the Bolivian Altiplano, further investigation showed precisely that such an inland sea exists on the edge of the Altiplano. Plato's 'sea', then, would appear to be the inland water called Lake Poopó.

Although Atlantis is famous as having sunk into the sea, and it may be easy to make a joke about 'how can Atlantis be in the Andes when it sank into the sea?' we must remember that Plato stated that Atlantis was on a level plain which was 'high above the level of the sea and enclosed by mountains'. Modern satellite mapping

Fig. 1.02. Model of the level rectangular plain, described in R.G. Bury's translation as: 'bordering on the sea and extending through the centre of the whole island'. (Critias 113C) It was 'originally a quadrangle, rectilinear for the most part, and elongated'. (Critias 118C, Bury 1929)

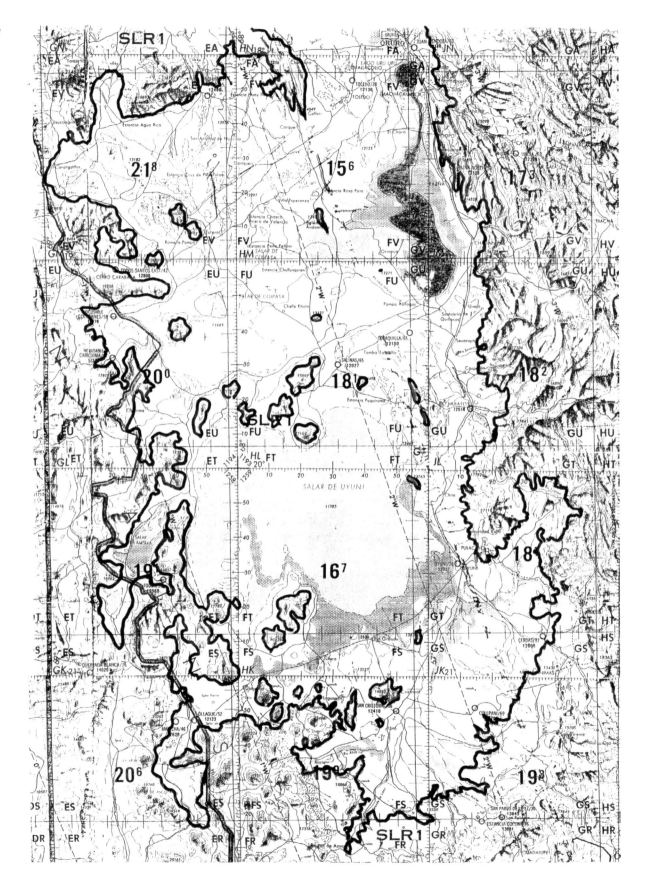

shows the Altiplano to be of rectangular configuration, perfectly level, enclosed on all sides by mountains, in an area subject to earthquakes and floods such as Plato said sank the city in a single day and night.

The whole area including the level plain (because it is a basin enclosed by mountains) has been submerged beneath the sea at successive intervals dating back thousands of years when the plain was covered with the waters of the giant paleolakes of which Lake Poopó is the last remnant, and in fact, at the date Plato gave, the plain was drowned first under the waters of paleolake Tauca, then after a dry spell of two thousand years, under the waters of paleo-lake Coipasa.

The discovery of the Andes solution

People often ask how I came to find the site in South America in the first place. In the beginning, I took an interest in reading books about ancient monuments like the Great Pyramid in Egypt, and Stonehenge, and became intrigued by the reference to ancient measurements, such as cubits. I was curious especially about the cubits which appear in the Bible in the description of Ezekiel's Temple where he sees the city (described again in St John) as: 'The holy city of God descending out of heaven'. The city measured on each side 500 reeds, the reed was a 'full great reed of six great cubits' making 3,000 cubits per side, yet it had a perimeter of '12,000 furlongs'. But he says he measured the wall twice, the second time as 'an hundred and forty-four cubits, according to the measure of a man', furthermore, 'the length and the breadth and the height of it were equal'.

This intrigued me so much that I entered into an exhaustive study of the origins of all the ancient measurement systems, among them the megalithic yard quoted by Professor A. Thom (Thom 1967) as being 32.64 inches, which he said was a standard unit of measurement used in the construction of ancient stone circles. I worked out that the megalithic yard was the distance travelled by

Fig. 1.03. On this satellite-derived navigation chart, the 13,000 ft (3,962 m) contour reveals the shape of the level, rectangular plain.

the planet Earth on its orbit in a 1/36,000th part of a second. The megalithic yard is therefore related to time and space and has no relationship to the geographic units such as the geographic foot or cubit or stade favoured by Plato. These last are all related to each other and are based upon the length of the minute of latitude of the observer — the geographic foot being a 1/6000th part of a minute of latitude and the geographic cubit counted as one and a half geographic feet, while the stade was usually counted as 600 geographic feet.

Then the penny dropped when I realized that Ezekiel said that he measured the city twice, once when it measured 500 great reeds and again when it measured 144 cubits 'according to the measure of a man'. I realized that he had measured it firstly in 'great' cubits of 30 inches then again in 'sacred' cubits of 25 inches. Therefore the wall measurement of 12,000 *furlongs* had been wrongly translated, because the four sides each measured 3,000 cubits, making a perimeter length of 12,000 *great cubits* not furlongs, but the wall of 144 cubits was measured in *sacred* cubits of 25 inches high, making a height of 3,600 inches or 300 feet.

I also realized that what Ezekiel had described was the tower and courtyard in Babylon since the tower was built in the form of a stepped pyramid and had a height of 300 feet and a base side of 300 feet — which was an ancient form of stade.

The difference between the 'geographic' cubits and the 'sacred' or 'great' cubits is that the geographic units are derived from the circumference of the Earth, which varies from place to place, because the Earth is not a perfect sphere, whereas the sacred and great cubits are derived from the polar diameter of the Earth which is a more scientific and even more ancient system of measurement.

So what difference does it make if a cubit has the value of 18.24 inches (geographic cubit), 19.8 inches (Sumerian cubit), 20.62 inches (Egyptian cubit) or 25 inches (sacred cubit) or 30 inches (great cubit)?

Well, since the geographic cubit was originally derived from the latitude of the observer, a Greek cubit being based on the latitude of Greece and an Egyptian cubit from the latitude of Egypt, it suggests that if a cubit of a certain length is found in some far off country, it might help trace the origins of some unknown prehistoric people, or travellers. To give an example of this, the so-called Sumerian yard of 33 inches has been found in other places of the world, notably Peru, and the standard width of an 'Incan' road was observed by Dr Ann Kendall (Kendall 1973) to be 16.5 feet — but there again,

16.5 feet is the standard length of a Sumerian surveying pole and an unexpected unit to be found in a country like South America which is supposedly not to have had any 'Old World' connections.

And who actually used the 25 inch 'sacred' cubit postulated as the length of the sacred cubit of the Bible? Again, the answer may well be found in Peru (Verrill 1953). And if this unit, or the ancient inch, as already outlined were derived from the dimensions of the Earth, it would suggest that our ancestors or 'Ancients' as they are sometimes called, or even megalithic man or someone at some ancient time was more mathematically advanced than we have been led to believe. The main question is this, if the inch is derived from the diameter of the Earth, and specifically as it turns out, from the polar diameter of the Earth, it begs the question — *who surveyed the Earth in the remote past?*

Like a mathematical equation, it is often the case that once a problem has been solved, the answer seems simple, but arriving at the answer may have been a long and arduous road.

So what has all that got to do with Atlantis? Well, I already mentioned that Plato told us the level rectangular plain of Atlantis measured 3,000 × 2,000 stades, and of course here we are thinking in Greek stades. But as the original measurements were made in Atlantis before coming to Egypt and then Athens, they would have been made in Atlantean units, so the plain and the canals which were said to be 100 feet wide or even one stade wide, could actually have been measured in different units unknown to us. It is useful to be aware, then, of other units of measurement which existed both in the Old World and the New.

All the same, the fact of Plato describing a plain of 3,000 × 2,000 stades for a missing island in the Atlantic Ocean awoke my interest in the Atlantis story and just as I methodically worked through the origins of all the ancient measurement units, I equally methodically set out to see if an island with a plain of 3,000 × 2,000 stades would actually fit in the Atlantic Ocean.

I should mention here that these days it is very popular for people to claim Atlantis to be just about anywhere, for example Crete, Andalucia and even Sicily were all mentioned at the Atlantis Conference 2008 and supporting diagrams were produced to prove these pet theories. But it is one thing to mark a rectangular plain on a small scale map and entirely different when you get a proper map at a large scale then anyone can verify that there is no rectangular plain of 3,000 × 2,000 stades, no matter what the unit of the stade, in either Crete, Andalucia or Sicily.

The next step with placing Plato's Atlantis in the Atlantic Ocean was to do what other people probably did. I drew out a rectangle based on Greek stades and studied some underwater profiles to see if it would fit in anywhere.

I even went as far as to draw a fictional island with a 3,000 × 2,000 stade plain, to see if that would fit in the Atlantic Ocean. And for a long time I remained with my fictional island with a fictional plain in the middle of the Atlantic Ocean, much the same as other people had done.

But then I came across books which suggested that Atlantis might have been in the Americas, specifically in the Andes, at Tiahuanacu, or Tiwanaku as it is now called, but that didn't seem quite right, as Atlantis was said to have a concentric ringed circular configuration, and to be located in the centre of the level rectangular plain. The next stage was to search all of the Americas for a place where a level, rectangular plain measuring 3,000 × 2,000 stades might fit in.

At that time, the topographical maps were not so clear as they are today, in defining the rectangular shape of the plain, but it seemed that in a region to the south of Tiwanaku, called the Altiplano, my Philips school atlas showed a smaller rectangular shaped area which might be a plain.

About that time, I had recently left the RAF where I had been working as a Photographic Interpreter as the job used to be called — in the modern jargon perhaps air photo analyst might be a better description — and I continued to work for a local authority in Cambridge as a cartographic draughtsman, so maps and map scales and models were no mystery to me, and it was off to Stanford's map shop in London to look for a better map of the region. This turned out to be the United States Air Force navigation chart at a scale of 1,000,000 which, being designed for the benefit of pilots, did not show in coloured form any rectangular level area such as Plato described. But it did have two distinct advantages, first, it included a grid of latitude and longitude, and second, and most important, it was derived from the latest satellite technology, and included delineating the land levels and elevations and heights of mountains etc.

Although other explorers such as Percy Fawcett have postulated that South America might be Atlantis, and Spanish historians such as Francisco López de Gómara (1552) or Pedro Sarmiento de Gamboa (1572) stated that South America was Atlantis (and I did not know that at the time), here I had the advantage of a technology that previous Atlantis researchers did not have at their disposal.

Now, as to the proof of Atlantis, the first proof is simply this. If it is to be Atlantis, it must have at its centre a level, rectangular shaped plain, preferably of 3,000 × 2,000 stades or in the proportions of 3,000 × 2,000 units. Due to my RAF training, although I had never previously actually built one, I began the preparation for the construction of a topographical model of the area. This meant tracing out, on a large sheet of drafting film, every single contour on the map, so that the contours could be subsequently cut out in polystyrene, to be successively built up and covered in modelling clay to give the correct topographical appearance.

It was when the contours reached the 13,000 ft level that the rectangular shape of the Altiplano jumped out at me, and it was then that I knew that here was the rectangular plain of Atlantis. Only instead of 3,000 × 2,000 Greek stades, it measured half that, in other words, 3,000 × 2000 stades of 300 feet instead of 600 feet. But then the Greek stade was a 1/10th of a minute of latitude whereas a 300 ft stade would be a 1/20th of a minute of latitude and that seemed a consolation since the Mayans and Aztecs had counted in twenties instead of tens. I don't expect the Greeks went there and measured everything in Greek stades, and if the story truly had come from Atlantis to Egypt then Greece, it would have been translated first from the Atlantean language into Egyptian, then into Greek.

So the important thing was that it was the largest perfectly level plain in the world and the map showed that it was rectangular and as Plato said, enclosed by mountains. That's right, Plato said it was enclosed by mountains, he never said there were no mountains on the southern side as is commonly shown, but *enclosed* by mountains and 'high above the level of the sea', another factor people take little account of.

> The part about the city was all a smooth plain,
> enclosing it round about, and being itself encircled by
> mountains which stretched as far as to the sea; and
> this plain had a level surface and was as a whole rec-
> tangular in shape ... (*Critias,* 118A, trans. Bury 1929)

> The city was surrounded by a uniformly flat plain,
> which was in turn enclosed by mountains which came
> right down to the sea. (Desmond Lee translation)

No other proposed Atlantis site in the world, whether above water or under water, has a level rectangular plain in the manner outlined and illustrated above.

Having built the model and discovered the site of the level plain in Bolivia, I felt it necessary to look for some other form of evidence on the ground which could provide proof of the new theory, or encourage others to take an interest in this new theory. But the archaeologists' response was negative. Sorry, no one interested.

I made contact with Professor Raymond Dart, famous for having discovered the 'missing link' in South Africa, a species of early man called 'Australopithecus'. Professor Dart lived in the USA, but I met him in the Churchill Hotel in London on one of his stopovers between USA and South Africa.

Deeply interested, he suggested I should contact Egerton Sykes, an Atlantis enthusiast who was then president of the British Chapter of the Explorers Club of New York. Sykes was at that time stepping down as president of the UK Chapter, so he in turn suggested I get in touch with his successor, Colonel John Blashford-Snell, famous for his expeditions to the source of the Blue Nile, and for world-girdling adventures with his young explorers in Operation Drake and Operation Raleigh. I made an appointment to meet the colonel in his office in London, part of the old War Office building.

Wishing to make a good impression, I paced up and down the street outside the building waiting for the appointed hour hoping to enter dead on time with 'military precision'.

I had not allowed enough time to get from the reception desk to his office which turned out to be on an upper floor, so arrived a few minutes late.

Then there was the choice of two doors, one marked 'Adjutant' and the other with the name of the colonel. I entered through the door with his name on it, which seemed only logical, 'Oh!' he said, 'you're supposed to come in through the other door, but everybody does that!'

In contrast to archaeologists, Colonel John Blashford-Snell or JBS as he is sometimes known, showed a keen interest in the subject. He had a simple philosophy — that if you did not go and have a look on the ground, you would never know for sure.

He was willing to take a group of his young explorers there, but in the end, owing to political difficulties in Bolivia and fearing for the safety of his Venturers, the plans had to be cancelled.

But then, just as is remarked in *The Celestine Prophecy* (Redfield 1977) that sometimes we meet people by coincidence which results in life-changing opportunities, years later in Cambridge, I did happen to meet an associate of JBS, Dr Frank Dawson who had participated in some expeditions in South America.

Frank offered to re-introduce me to the colonel and since I had by that time some small scale Landsat photos which seemed to show a section of giant canal similar to one Plato described for Atlantis, JBS offered to go and 'have a look' on a recce.

Months later, his report came in. He had been to the area, hired a jeep, driven up and down but found nothing. That seemed strange, since to me, it was clear there was something there on the satellite photo and consequently should be there in the ground in Bolivia. So it was time to jump on a plane to Bolivia to 'have a look for myself'.

It meant travelling to a town called Oruro on the edge of the level, rectangular plain and hiring a jeep, but this proved impossible on my first try because I had altitude sickness so had to return to La Paz.

I was persuaded to go back and have another go, this time by a Bolivian archaeologist, Ponce Sanguines who lived in La Paz and, like JBS, suggested that the only way to find out for sure was to go there myself.

So it was back to Oruro and no easy matter to navigate across the salt desert but there it was, the great channel running across the landscape and it even had water in it — supplied by underground springs and the locals used it to water their flocks of llamas.

I felt quite elated to have found such a channel so this time I sent off a 'report' to JBS, being the only one I had found taking any interest in a possible Atlantis in Bolivia.

As Professor Raymond Dart had pointed out, it would be necessary for some independent person to go to Bolivia to verify the presence of any canal or other Atlantis-related discoveries.

In fact, JBS had already informed me of a Mediterranean-style amphora to be found in the museum in Oruro: 'Just like hundreds I have seen on dives in the Mediterranean,' he said.

Then eventually he came up with the proposal to commission some reed boats to be built and to sail them along the river Desaguadero from Lake Titicaca to Lake Poopó to show the river could have been used for ancient purposes of trade, then to continue down to have a look at the great canal west of Lake Poopó.

So in 1998 I found myself back in Bolivia, this time with a film crew for the BBC making an Atlantis film and with a date to rendezvous with JBS's Kota Mama expedition. Around this time also, my book *Atlantis: the Andes Solution* was published, setting out the theory of Atlantis in Bolivia.

Pushing on ahead, I managed to locate the giant channel in the desert, and the team and jeep came straggling up. But afterwards one of the army captains attached to the expedition pronounced that it was a fault line and not a canal, so the disappointed film crew jetted off down to a lower region called the Beni where Clark Erickson had found hundreds of man-made mounds, interconnected with thousands of straight line channels, that is, canals, which had previously been dismissed as 'fault lines'.

Years later, I met Carlos Abecia in Cochabamba, a former chief of the Bolivian Geological Survey who examined the air photos of the giant canal feature and stated definitively, that in his opinion, it was *not* a fault line, but originally a man-made channel.

There followed an interlude of several years of expeditions, visiting sites around the Altiplano looking for volcanoes with circular concentric rings and visiting such outlandish places as Pumiri, an 'enchanted' or 'petrified' city of stone formations on the northern edge of the Altiplano.

Here, men were said to have lived like troglodytes in caves and all around us were weathered sculptures in the form of Condors, Bears and other animals from some prehistoric times — including a *bison* — an animal thought not to have existed in South America.

Then there was Volcán Quemado, on the far west of the Altiplano — a formation consisting of 'nesting' craters, that is to say, one crater inside another crater; and Volcán Columna — a crater caused by an explosion of gas, the rim of the crater being the remnant that fell back to earth.

Also there was a visit to the Chipaya — an extremely remote village on the edge of the Salar de Coipasa — extremely difficult to get to or to return from, but home to the 'Uru Chipaya' people. These are said to be amongst the oldest original inhabitants of South America and very reminiscent of the ancient Sumerians, having formerly lived in reed houses and constructed the reed boats still found today on Lake Titicaca. They are also said to be people from an ancient time of darkness.

So was established what I began to call 'The Atlantis Trail', leading to the inspection of another volcano at a site called Santuario de Quillacas, this time more in the centre of the level rectangular plain, which was, after all, where Plato had said the city was located.

But it seemed so hard to believe that Plato's description could be so exactly right, and instead of following his precise instructions and perhaps misled by the satellite images, I had been looking all over the place.

But then Plato did say the island 'sank into the sea and disappeared' so I wasn't really expecting to find it on dry land, and there again, 'in the centre of the plain, 50 stades from the sea' seems simple to understand, but 'centre of the plain' could also be interpreted in different ways.

As a result of an invitation to Bolivia by Carlos Aliaga of Cochabamba, I found myself arriving at Santuario de Quillacas in an old Toyota jeep and moments later Carlos came rushing out of the church announcing that it was made of 'red, black and white stones' — 'Just like in Atlantis!' he exclaimed.

On the way over to Quillacas we had seen another interesting volcano in the distance — called Pampa Aullagas — with a band of white running round its summit and reminding me of a wedding cake, but we had no time to visit it on that expedition.

Back in England, I received an email from Carlos telling me he had been back to the other site, and that it did have channels 'going up the mountain like an ascending sine wave'.

Shortly afterwards I had attracted the attention of the Discovery Channel who wanted to make a documentary, so it was back to Bolivia once more, this time visiting the site at Pampa Aullagas. Since actual ruined cities make better TV material, we also filmed the site at Tiwanaku which by orders of the high masters back at Discovery Channel, they had been told to include.

At that time, being the first time on site at Pampa Aullagas there was not time to study it properly or survey it properly, film crews always being in a hurry, so the remainder of this book takes off where the story with the Discovery Channel left off in the year 2000.

The day before leaving Bolivia in March 2001, I met with Dr Mario Montaño Aragón who mentioned in passing that Pampa Aullagas was the 'home of the water god'. I did not know then the name of the water god in Bolivian legend. It turned out that in 'The Legend of the Desaguadero' (the story of a city punished by the Gods and sunk in the sea), the water god 'Pachacamac' is sent sailing down the Desaguadero River to finally disappear in the waters of Aullagas (Lake Poopó).

The other name for the water god was Tunupa and — as explained by Lynn Sikkink and Braulio Choque from the village of Huari on the opposite side of the lake to Pampa Aullagas — Tunupa appeared in different guises, the legends varying from village to village. It also seems that Tunupa was an Aymara god dating back to the sixteenth century and perhaps before that of Puquina origin. He was associated with water and sometimes described as the maker of water and travelled along the water axis from Lake Titicaca to Lake Poopó where he disappeared in the region of Pampa Aullagas. At this point, the story continues with Tunupa being deposited on the shore of the lake in the guise of a beautiful woman, now known as Thunapa in the female form, who subsequently married a male god on the peak opposite — Azanaques — an echo of Plato's story of Poseidon marrying Cleito who lived on a hill. Thunapa subsequently runs away from Azanaques and in doing so 'lays down' at Pampa Aullagas thus creating the ringed formation there.

So I think here we have the origins of the Atlantis story with the level plain, the involvement of the god of the sea, and so on, but it is from this point on that the story is more difficult to prove. Was there ever a city as Plato described it, with perfectly circular rings of land and interconnecting harbours, and how much of the story was Plato's invention for political purposes? Jules Verne in his novel *Twenty Thousand Leagues under the Seas* painted the picture of a Greek-style Atlantis sunk beneath the waves where divers could walk around in the remains of Greek-style temples, and this image has stayed with people ever since. But the historical reality is more likely to have been an Andean city, perhaps like Machu Picchu or even a floating village of the Uru.

Some people believe every single word of Plato's account to be true, while other people believe every single word to be totally false. Plato himself said the basis of the story was a true story which was brought from Egypt and which he intended to build upon at the Festival of Athena and although he repeats three times that it was a true story, there always remains the element of doubt due to the philosophical nature of his writings.

The test of any theory is first to write the theory, then to see if the observations fit the premises of the theory. The Altiplano is the only site that fits practically all of the *geographic points* of Plato's description. Clearly we have geographical evidence, geological evidence and mythical evidence from Bolivia, as well as the fact that the level plain is itself eminently suitable for the water canal based culture Plato described, and the water canal culture continues to this day. So what we need to do next is to look at the key features of Plato's description and see to what extent they correspond with the geographical reality on the ground. Most of the following aspects will be examined in more detail throughout the book.

The canals

One of the key features described by Plato, was a large canal said to be one stade wide which ran around the perimeter of the level plain and a system of smaller canals parallel to each other which criss-crossed the plain at regular intervals. These were joined by intersecting canals at right angles and used for transportation by boats of the season's products.

Looking for evidence of a canals system on the Altiplano has been an important focus in the search for evidence. Satellite images showed a very large channel similar to the giant canal which Plato described just to the west of Lake Poopó, and when this was visited on site, it still had water in the base due to the fact that the channel was supplied by water from wells drawing water from underground sources.

Recent high resolution satellite imagery shows the area just south of Oruro and bordering on Lake Poopó to be completely covered in a system of parallel canals similar to Plato's description.

Canals are certainly a feature of the area, which still suffers today from alternating drought and flooding. These smaller canals appear to be about 5 ft (1.5 m) wide and have interconnecting transverse channels whilst some exist in a chequerboard pattern and even extend under the River Desaguadero and what is now Lake UruUru (part of Lake Poopó).

The island of concentric rings

The most distinguishing feature of Atlantis (and one which even the Milos Atlantis conference 2005 doubted might exist) was that the main island of Atlantis which Plato described first of all as the home of Poseidon and later as the site where the city of the descendants of Atlas reigned, comprised a central island *surrounded by alternating rings of land and water.* In Plato's words:

> There were two rings of land, and three of water,
> which he turned as with a lathe, each having its cir-
> cumference equidistant every way from the centre.

And:

> Near the plain, over against its centre, at a distance of
> about 50 stades (from the sea) there stood a mountain
> that was low on all sides. (*Critias,* 113C)

It took five expeditions on the Bolivian Altiplano following the Atlantis Trail to find a location that matched Plato's mountain, which was low on all sides and in the centre of the plain next to the sea. This site, at the southern end of Lake Poopó, is called Pampa Aullagas.

The central island which was '5 stades' in diameter lies in the centre of the level rectangular plain, 50 stades from the sea and is enclosed by a volcanic low plateau containing three concentric sandy channels which formerly held water, separated by rings of land.

The surrounding plain has sunk in elevation and the nearby inland sea has receded leaving the island as a volcano on dry land.

In the wet season, Pampa Aullagas becomes an island and before the sinking of the surrounding plain, the water from the lake could have entered the volcano, filling the natural depressions making circular canal-like harbours and in fact, around 11,500 BC the waters of Lake Poopó (known as paleolake Tauca) were at the correct level to enter the volcano creating circular rings of water.

In terms of the length and breadth of the surrounding rectangular plain, (which Plato said measured $3,000 \times 2,000$ stades) the 'stade' would appear to have a value of around half a Greek stade that is, in round numbers around 300ft (91.4 m) as can be determined by measuring in the manner Plato said, across the plain from the sea at its widest point.

In terms of the site at Pampa Aullagas, the 'best fit' has been a 'stade' of 165 ft (50 m), which would be 100 Sumerian cubits of 19.8 inches (502.92 mm).

The metals

Amongst the numerous features mentioned by Plato, we should particularly mention the metals. The walls of the city were said to

*Fig. 1.04. Location of the Atlantis site at
Pampa Aullagas, south of Lake Poopó.*

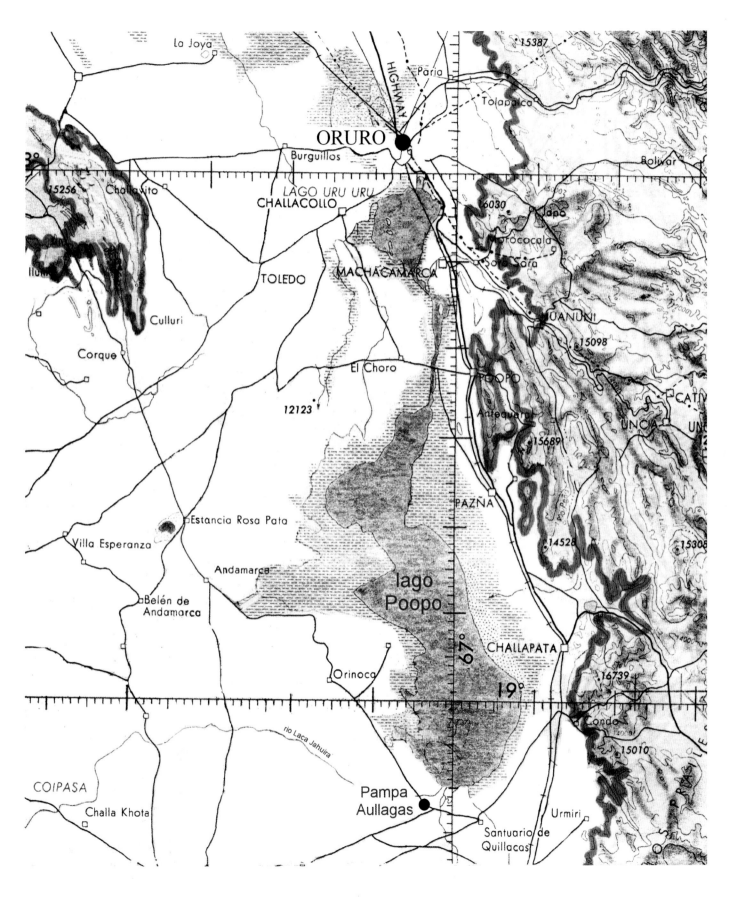

be plated in metals which to us were rare and valuable, but to the original inhabitants were common and plentiful. Amongst these were gold, silver, copper, tin and a mysterious alloy called 'orichalcum' which one translator, Sir Desmond Lee, considered to be 'a completely imaginary metal'. R.G. Bury considered it might have been 'mountain copper'. This metal which has puzzled people most of all, could be polished and then 'sparkled like fire'*, as Plato says: 'there being mines of it in many places of the island — I mean 'orichalcum', which was the most precious of the metals then known, except gold'. (*Critias,* 114E)

> And they covered with brass† as though with a plaster, all of the circumference of the wall which surrounded the outermost circle; and that of the inner one they coated with tin; and that which encompassed the acropolis itself with orichalcum which sparkled like fire. (*Critias,* 116B)

> All the exterior of the temple they coated with silver, save only the pinnacles, and these they coated with gold. As to the interior, they made the roof all of ivory in appearance, variegated with gold and silver and orichalcum, and all the rest of the walls and pillars and floors they covered with orichalcum. And they placed therein golden statues ... and outside, round about the temple, there stood images in gold of all the princes ... (*Critias,* 116D)

Now, of course, the main motivation for the Spanish Conquest of the continent was the abundance of precious metals to be found there. Among the indigenous people, gold was not used as a currency; it was valued more for its colour and beauty, gold being the 'sweat of the sun' and silver being the 'tears of the moon'. The gold of Peru is already famous in the world, and the silver from the mines in Potosi in Bolivia was a rich fountain of wealth which drove forward the Spanish Empire. Next to the mountain of silver in Potosi there is another mountain of tin, which is also a rare metal

---

* 'Red fire' in Jowett's translation.
† 'Bronze' in Lee's translation.

not found in many places in the world. We might well conclude that this is the place described by Plato where he says: 'The wealth they possessed was so great that the like will never easily be seen again'. (*Critias,* 114D)

Indeed, right around the edge of Lake Poopó and the Atlantis site at Pampa Aullagas we have all the metals mentioned by Plato, the largest gold mine in Bolivia at La Joya, the mountain of solid silver at Potosi, tin mines at Huanuni, tin and silver at Oruro, and a natural mine of orichalcum at Urukilla. So in fact an alloy of gold and copper alloy matching Plato's description exists in the Andes, where it is called *tumbaga.*

When the gold/copper alloy is heated then the object immersed in a solution of alum, the copper dissolves from the surface to leave an object with the appearance of pure gold. The object can then be polished to consolidate the gold atoms on the surface and further enhance the sparkling, golden appearance. Variations in colour are also possible, since the more copper in the gold/copper ratio, the more red the final appearance.

Here is what Karen Olsen Bruhns, writing in *Ancient South America* has to say about it:

> Copper and copper alloy objects were routinely gilded or silvered, the original colour apparently not being much valued. The gilded copper objects were

Fig. 1.05. An axe head of 'orichalcum' — mixture of gold and copper with a small amount of arsenic — the surface has darkened due to oxidization of the copper.

often made of an alloy which came to be very important in all of South and Central American metallurgy: *tumbaga*. This is a gold-copper alloy which is significantly harder than copper, but which retains its flexibility when hammered. It is thus ideally suited to the formation of elaborate objects made of hammered sheet metal. In addition, it casts well and melts at a lower temperature than copper, always a consideration when fuel sources for a draught were the wind and men's lungs. The alloy could be made to look like pure gold by treatment of the finished face with an acid solution to dissolve the copper, and then by hammering or polishing to join the gold, giving a uniformly gold surface. (Bruhns 1994)

The process was further explained and demonstrated by Adam Hart-Davis in his programme 'What The Ancients Did For Us' screened by the Open University (BBC2), March 2, 2005. Taking a small piece of *tumbaga* consisting of fifty percent gold and fifty percent copper, the alloy was hammered into the shape of a miniature mask suitable for mounting on a finger ring. At this stage it looked like polished copper before being annealed by heating with a torch to a cherry-red colour at a temperature of 500°.

The alloy was then quenched in water whereby it turned black due to the copper on the surface oxidizing and turning into copper oxide on top of the gold.

The alloy was then immersed in a hot solution of alum whereupon, as in some ancient alchemical process, the copper oxide dissolved away revealing a shining surface of 'the most noble of the metals looking like pure gold'.

So there is nothing 'imaginary' about orichalcum.

Hot and cold springs

Hot and cold springs were a feature of Atlantis and used for public baths.

> The springs they made use of, one kind being of cold, another of warm water, were of abundant volume ...

and, moreover, they set reservoirs round about, some under the open sky, and others under cover to supply hot baths in the winter. (*Critias*, 117A)

Hot and cold springs also exist all over the Altiplano.

Earthquakes

Earthquakes were a major factor in the destruction of Atlantis and there is evidence of earthquake destruction on the site at Pampa Aullagas as well as around the surrounding Altiplano

The red, black and white stones

Another important factor which may be easily demonstrated on this site is that Plato mentioned that the buildings were made of red, black and white stones, intermixed to give a pleasing appearance. All three colours of stone are to be found at Pampa Aullagas, some looking as if they are fragments from stones used in former buildings though no ancient buildings themselves remain.

Local legend

Most remarkable of all, as we saw earlier, a Bolivian legend called *The Legend of the Desaguadero* tells of a city on the edge of a lake. It falls into evil ways and in exactly the same manner as Plato's city is punished by the gods and submerged by the sea. In the Greek legend, the name of the god of the sea who created the rings of water and land in Atlantis was Poseidon, but in Bolivian legend, the god of the sea is called *Tunupa* in the Aymara language, and in Quechua (language of the Incas) he is called Pachacamac, or Viracocha. According to Bolivian legend it was Tunupa (the sea god) who created the ringed formation at Pampa Aullagas. Not only that, but Tunupa is said to have disappeared beneath the waters of Lake Poopó near Pampa Aullagas.

In Plato's version, the wife of Poseidon had five pairs of twin sons (*Critias*, 113E) and in Inca legend, after a great flood, Viracocha 'adopted' five pairs of sons.

The sixteenth century Inca historian Guaman Poma de Ayala tells us the first inhabitants were born in pairs. Additionally, the Aymara kingdoms which existed on the Altiplano also existed in pairs, so there can be no doubt that the story of Atlantis has strong echoes from a Bolivian legend. We look at the background of local legend and ancient history in more detail in Chapters 3–5.

Naming of the continent

We also have evidence in the manner of the naming of the continent itself. The continent had remained lost from European knowledge until 1492 when rediscovered by Christopher Columbus sailing west in an attempt to reach the Indies. Columbus had with him a map and believed he had reached what he called the 'Indias'.

In 1507 the German cartographer Waldseemuller produced a map of the newly found continent. He decided to name the continent 'America' in honour of the navigator Amerigo Vespucci who was first to recognize that the continent was a continent in its own right, a 'New World', instead of being part of Asia as Columbus had thought (see Chapter 2).

So the newly discovered continent came to be called America, but at the same time many people thought that what Christopher Columbus had in fact discovered was Atlantis. The first book to mention this was *La Historia de las Indias* by Francisco López de Gómara. Published in 1552, the book was banned the following year and not reprinted until 1727.

The next book to state definitively that South America was Atlantis was *La Historia de los Incas* written by the great historian and classical scholar Pedro Sarmiento de Gamboa following an official inquest into the true history of the Incas with the backing of the Viceroy of Peru. Sarmiento de Gamboa's book clearly states that South America was Atlantis and at the time he was writing was known by the names of 'the Western Indies of Castile or America also called Atlanticus or the Atlantic Island'. So the continent was also known sometimes as 'New Castile', 'New Spain' or 'Atlanticus', then latterly, 'America'. In 1572 Sarmiento de Gamboa's book was sent to Philip II, king of Spain, and never heard of again, being lost for three hundred years until it was discovered in a library in Germany in 1893 and republished in 1906 (see below Chapter 4).

Only many years after starting my research did I find Sarmiento de Gamboa's book. It is an extremely difficult book to get hold of, although there is a modern English translation, and they did not even have a copy in the British Library. But they had two copies in Cambridge University Library. Alas, in these great and free democratic days, I was not allowed entry, not being a member of the University. I was told I would need a reference from a doctor or a priest. A friend of mine sent me a copy instead from Madrid.

Now the Atlantis Island remained a popular name and was shown as such on maps made by the French cartographer Guillermo Sanson in Paris in 1661. But then following the Declaration of Independence by the United States in 1776, the name 'America' became universally adopted and the name of Atlantis forgotten until resurrected in modern times. No attention was given to the fact

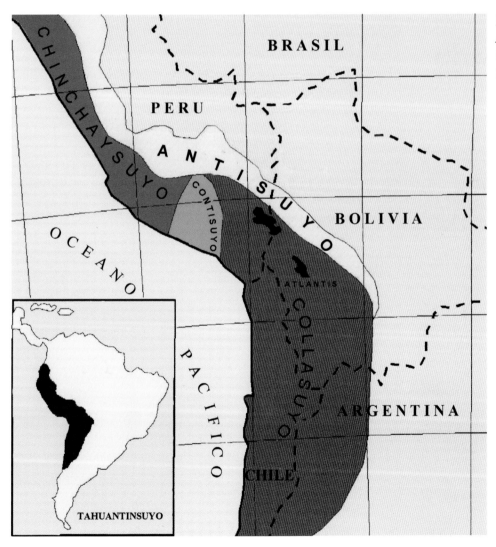

Fig. 1.06. Location of Atlantis and Antisuyo in the empire of Tahuantinsuyo.

Fig. 1.07. Antis Indians of Peru, 1869.

that the southern continent already had an indigenous name given by the Incas before the Conquest. Their name for the continent was 'Tahuantinsuyo' meaning 'Land of the Four Quarters'. One of these quarters was called 'Antisuyo' meaning 'the kingdom of the Antis'.

Antis is an Inca word meaning 'copper' which could refer to the abundance of copper on the continent or the people themselves who are also copper-coloured, and an indigenous tribe living to this day on the eastern slopes of Peru is known as the 'Antis'. The very name of the Andes themselves is also thought to be a corruption of the word 'Antis'.

'Atl' is an Aztec word meaning 'water' and the combination of 'atl' and 'antis' an excellent name for this continent since large parts of it are in fact under water in the wet season with severe flooding throughout Amazonia and Beni regions.

If it hadn't been called 'Atlantis', it might have been called 'Umasuyo', 'uma' meaning 'water' and 'suyo' meaning 'kingdom' in the Aymara language, or perhaps 'Aymara Omasuyu' which is the proposed Aymara name for the country.

Elephants

> Moreover it contained a very large stock of elephants ...
> (*Critias,* 114E)

A frequently read comment is that there were no elephants in South America, but in fact there were mastodons, which is a species of elephant, and remains of mastodons may be seen in the museum in Tarija to the south east of the Altiplano.

Animal sacrifice

> In the sacred precincts of Poseidon there were bulls at large; and the ten princes ... whatsoever bull they captured they led up to the pillar and cut its throat over the top of the pillar, raining down blood on the inscription ... when they were consecrating all the limbs of the bull, they mixed a bowl of wine and poured in on behalf of each one a gout of blood, and

the rest they carried to the fire ... and after this they
drew out from the bowl with golden ladles, and making libation over the fire... (*Critias,* 119E)

Towards the end of the tale, Plato recounts how the ten kings of
Atlantis gathered in the precincts of the temple of Poseidon every
fifth and every sixth year to pass laws and make judgements. This
they did in a special ceremony around a pillar of orichalcum which
contained the written laws and deeds of the first princes.

In the precincts of the temple were said to be bulls running at
large, and the kings captured a bull with a stave and a noose and led
the animal up to the pillar where they cut its throat over the top of
the pillar raining blood down on the inscription. Then they mixed
blood with wine in a bowl and drew from it with golden ladles,
drinking a toast, and swearing to observe the sacred laws written on
the pillar before consuming the remainder of the blood in the fire.

Well, one might argue that there were no bulls in South America
prior to their introduction by the *conquistadores.* But one could
equally argue that there were no llamas in Athens either! So in
translation, the word 'bull' may well have been adopted for 'llama'.
Plato stated that he gave all the original names Greek equivalents 'to
make it more agreeable to his readers'. It is important to remember
that he never actually visited the site himself and neither the ancient
Greeks nor ancient Egyptians had probably ever seen or heard of a
llama, thus 'bull' was substituted, just as 'trireme' was substituted
for whichever type of ship or boat was originally used.

Llama sacrifice is an ancient tradition in the Andes. Garcilaso de
la Vega, the half-Indian Spanish chronicler records the details of the
great celebration of the winter solstice in Cuzco. The Inca king rose
to his feet and took two gold cups which they filled with beverages
inviting the sun and the Inca relatives to drink. Then the Inca priests
brought a quantity of llamas, and beginning with a black llama
because that was the preferred colour for sacrifice, they carried out
the ritual sacrifice, burning the blood and the hearts in the sacred
fire. The celebration lasted nine days with music, food and dancing
in honour of their god, the sun (Vega 1609).

The sacrifice of llamas in special ceremonies continues in Bolivia
up to this day. When Lonnie Thompson, a paleoclimatologist from
the Byrd Polar Research Centre led a fifty strong expedition to
Nevada Sajama in 1998, he had to take part in a local ceremony
before being able to haul his drilling equipment to the summit of

the mountain. The villagers and expedition members gathered in a circle around a fire, then two holy men laid a white llama on a stone and slit its throat. Offering songs and prayers to the earth-goddess Pachamama, they then burned figurines in the fire and sprinkled the llama's blood on the sand.

Two crops per year

> They cropped the land twice a year, making use of
> the rains from heaven in the winter, and the waters
> that issue from the earth in summer, by conducting
> the streams from the trenches. (*Critias,* 118C)

In areas around Lake Titicaca where the now mostly abandoned canalized field systems have been restored, two crops a year have been possible with greatly increased yields. This is due to the increased localized temperatures created by the heat retained in the water, also the sediments from the canals when heaped up on the land plots provide additional nutrients.

Recent developments

Recent events have overturned previous conceptions about the ancient history of South America (for background on all of the following, see References and Sources). In August 2004, the international Akakor expedition discovered ancient walls dating from 4000 BC submerged under Lake Titicaca at a depth of 120 m (394 ft). There is also the recent discovery of pyramids at Caral in Peru which date to 2627 bc, contemporary with the oldest pyramids in Egypt and older than Cheops' Great Pyramid in Egypt. Even more recently, remains of a 5,500 year old plaza have been found at Caral.

Mummies found near Arica in Chile are also older than the oldest mummies in Egypt (see Chapter 3).

Urban settlements have recently been proven to have existed throughout all of Amazonia in areas thought of as only pristine jungle.

On the shores of Lake Titicaca has been found a fossilized human footprint thought to date back five to fifteen million years.

Also on the shores of Lake Titicaca was discovered a large stone dish known as the *Fuente Magna* and covered in proto-Sumerian cuneiform writing (see Chapter 5).

Expeditions are presently underway to investigate a 5 mile (8 km) diameter meteorite crater in the Beni region of Bolivia (Blashford-Snell 2008) which it is thought may have impacted between five and thirty thousand years ago and contributed to the extinction of several ancient civilizations throughout Amazonia. One cannot help wonder whether this may also have been the event which triggered the collapse of the 'Atlantis' civilization on the Altiplano.

Although the geographic description of Atlantis clearly belongs to South America, the description of horses, chariots, the fleet of ships, and so on, is somewhat more problematical.

Fossilized remains of horses have recently been found in Peru, but these are of the smaller variety.

We must remember Plato's stated objective in the Atlantis story, which was to find a suitable enemy which could be seen to be defeated by his ancient city of Athens, or ideal state, and note also that it was not Atlantis which was the ideal state, but a theoretical version of Athens (*Timaeus,* 19C, 20B, 20D).

It may be then that, as the writer Robert Graves thought, elements of other ancient legends were grafted on to the Atlantis description (Graves 1955).

So Atlantis becomes a great power, with 10,000 chariots and 1,200 ships (*Critias,* 119B), although again I would mention that 1,200 was the number of ships sent against Troy. In the end, then, the story, as well as the geographic description of South America, has elements both of the 'Sea Peoples' as the confederated nations, and Troy as the finest of the deeds the Athenians accomplished.

The dating

The dating is a difficult question, some factors point to an early date, such as the mastodons mentioned above, yet Plato tells us that 'nine thousand is the sum of years since the war occurred' and he is describing the foundation of Athens and the 'finest of the deeds the Greeks achieved'. Another problem arises since Plato gave the same date for the foundation of Atlantis, as he did for its destruction.

If we substitute lunar 'years' for solar years, Plato's comment would bring the date down to around 1260 BC and the period of the Trojan war, which might correspond to the 'finest of the deeds the Greeks achieved'.

Atlantis was said to have been a confederation of nations that controlled Libya, meaning North Africa, up to the borders of Egypt and Europe as far as Tuscany. So the 'confederated nations attempting to enslave the eastern Mediterranean' which Plato described could have been what are usually called 'the Sea Peoples' who attacked Egypt in 1220 and 1186 bc, attempting to enter Egypt by sea and also with land armies entering via Libya and Palestine, all of which were defeated by the Egyptian pharaohs.

Without going so far as to say the Sea Peoples came from South America, I would point out that it is not known for certain where all of them actually came from, and drawings made of those taken prisoner by the Egyptians show them as wearing tall feathered head-dresses similar to Amazonian Indians.

Traces of coca and tobacco have also been found in the remains of Egyptian mummies of this period (see References and Sources) and it seems possible that the story of Atlantis may have been brought to Greece from Egypt as Plato claimed, having arrived in Egypt through captive warriors of 'the Sea Peoples', or maybe the traders who first brought American products to Egypt.

Fig. 1.08. Comparison of head-gear of Amazonian Indians and an 'Atalante' warrior from Tula, Mexico to the high feather head-dresses of the Sea Peoples.

2. The Great Secret of the Indias

We must remember that South America is a country which had its history destroyed by the invading Europeans in a conquest carried out in the name of the Church and in the pursuit of gold and other riches, where the original inhabitants were deprived of their lands, taken from their agricultural environment and sent down the mines in pursuit of what the Europeans deemed a precious metal, while in Mexico the books of their ancestors were burned and in Peru the ruling nobility were eliminated, including those people specially trained to remember their ancestral history.

So our investigation into the ancient past and legend of South America has to try and find a way past this deliberate destruction of its old traditions and beliefs. However, the identification of South America as Atlantis seems to have been clear to some of the European writers of the time.

Pedro Sarmiento de Gamboa, the Spanish historian who wrote extensively about the history of the Incas, was not apparently, the first to suggest that South America was Atlantis. Francisco López de Gómara, an ordained priest who as private and domestic chaplain in 1540 entered the service of Hernando Cortés, conqueror of Mexico, is usually credited with being the first person to recognize South America as Atlantis, writing in his book *La Historia de las Indias* — the 'History of the Indies' — or to give it its full title, *Hispania Victrix; First and Second Parts of the General History of the Indies, with the whole discovery and notable things that have happened since they were acquired until the year 1551, with the conquest of Mexico and New Spain,* published at Zaragoza in 1552.

Unlike Sarmiento de Gamboa, Francisco López de Gómara never actually visited America (or so it is said, though other reports say he spent four years in Mexico as secretary to Cortés) and relied for his information on *conquistadores* returning to Europe.

The first part of the book is dedicated to the Emperor Charles V: 'To Don Carlos, Emperor of Romans, King of Spain, Lord of the Indies and New World, the whole discovery and conquest of the Antilles, Peru, Chile and Central America'. The second part of the book, 'Chronicle of the Conquest of New Spain', deals with the conquest of Mexico and Peru.

The book was banned by Prince Philip (later Philip II) in 1553 and the ban not removed until 1727 when it was included in a collection of work of early historians by Don Andreas Gonzalez Martial — *Colección de Historiadores Primitivos de las Indias Occidentales* (Collection of Work by Early Historians of the Western Indies)

A rare and little known work, Gómara's account of the discovery of the Indies is charmingly written and since it offers a deeper insight into how Columbus, or Cristóbal Colón as he was called, came to discover the Indies, I have included part of it below:

XIII. The First Discovery of the Indies

> Navigating a caravel in the Ocean sea there was such a strong and continuous east wind that they came to a stop in a land unknown and unmarked on any navigation chart. They returned from there in many more days than it took to arrive; and when they did arrive there were left no more than the pilot and another three or four mariners, who, as they arrived sick of hunger and work, died after a short time in the port. We relate here how were found the Indies by those unfortunates who saw them first, who then gave up the life without enjoying the benefits of their discovery and without leaving, at least a memory of how they were called, nor where they were, neither in which year they were found ... Neither are we left the name of this pilot, and everything comes to a final end with death. Some say the pilot was Andaluz, with contracts in the Canaries and the Madeiras when this long and fatal navigation took place; others say he was Vizcaino, with contracts in England and France; and others Portuguese, who went to or came from la Mina or India, which squares well with the name which they took and gave to this new land.
>
> Also there are those who say that the caravel put in at Portugal, and who say also at Madeira or another of the Azores; however nothing is affirmed. Only everyone agrees that this pilot died in the house of Cristóbal Colón, in whose possession remained the papers of the caravel the story of all this long voyage, with the range and latitude of the lands newly seen and discovered.

XIV. Who Cristóbal Colón was

Cristóbal Colón was native of Cugureo, or as some wish, of Nervi, village of Genova, distinguished city of Italy. He was descended, as some say, from the Pelestreles of Placencia of Lombardy. He began from a small age to be a mariner, a position which occupies many from the coast of Genova; and thus he spent many years in Syria and other parts of the East.

Then he became a master in the making of navigation charts, something he was born for. He came to Portugal to take account of the southern coast of Africa and those coasts where the Portuguese sailed in order to better make and sell his charts. He married in that kingdom, or, as many say, in the island of Madeira, where I think he lived at the time when the aforementioned caravel arrived.

He accommodated the ship's master in his house, who subsequently told him of the voyage which had taken place and the new lands which he had seen, so that he could put them on a new chart which he would then buy. In this comedy the pilot then died leaving (Colón) the account, course and altitude of the new lands, and thus Cristóbal Colón took notice of the Indies.

Others also wish to say, because everyone says so, that Cristóbal Colón was a good Latin and Cosmographer, and that he was motivated to look for the land of the Antipodes, and the rich Cipango (Japan) of Marco Polo, having read Plato in the *Timaeus* and the *Critias,* where it speaks of the great Atlantis island and a hidden land greater than Asia and Africa; and in Aristotles or Teofrasto, in the Book of Marvels, which says that certain Carthaginian merchants, navigating the strait of Gibraltar to the west and midlatitudes, discovered, at the end of many days, a great unpopulated island, full of provisions and with navigable rivers; and which was understood by many of the previous authors by my annotations.

Cristóbal Colón was not an educated person, but understood well. And as he took notice of these new

lands on account of the dead pilot, he informed himself of learned men about what the ancients said concerning other lands and worlds. More than others he
communicated with a friar Juan Pérez de Marchena,
who dwelt in the monastery of La Rábida; and thus,
he was very certain in that which the pilot said and
wrote who died in his house.

It seems to me that if Colón were to reach by scientific methods where the Indies were located, that
much earlier, and without coming to Spain, he would
be able to deal with the Genoese, who run all round
the world to gain something, to go and find something. Therefore no-one thought of such a thing until
encountering this Spanish pilot who by fortune of the
sea discovered them ...

*XVII. The honour and favours bestowed on Colón by the
Catholic Kings for having discovered the Indies*

The Catholic Kings were in Barcelona when Colón
disembarked in Palos, and he had to go there.
Moreover the road was long and he was hindered by a
lot of rain, he was very honoured and famous, because
everyone came out to see him on the road for having
discovered another world, and bringing from there
great riches and men of a new form, colour and dress.

Some said that he had discovered the forbidden
navigation of the Carthaginians; others, that which
Plato, in *Critias,* took for lost in the storm and mud
in the sea;

They put Cristóbal Colón around the coat of arms
on which they conceded the following lettering:

For Castille and for León
A New World discovered Colón

XVIII. Why they are called Indians

Before we go further I would like to say my opinion
about this name Indies, because some believe that
they are so called because our men of the Indies are

of the same colour as the Eastern Indies. It appears to me that they differ greatly in colour and in features. It is true that from India they call them Indies. India properly speaking is that great province of Asia where Alexander the Great made war, which takes its name from the river Indus, and which is divided into many kingdoms and regions. From this great India, which we also call Oriental, came forth great companies of men, and they came (according to Herodotus) to populate Ethiopia, which is between the Bermejo Sea and the Nile, and which today belongs to Prester John.

They stayed so long there, in that land with its ancient customs and name in which they worked; and thus, Ethiopia was called India: and for this many say, amongst them Aristotle and Seneca, that India was near Spain.

From India then, that of Prester John, where the Portuguese were, is called our Indies, because the caravel was either coming from or going to there which with time inevitably carried them off; and as the pilot saw these new lands he called them Indies, and thus they were always called by Cristóbal Colón. Those who have a great knowledge of Cristóbal Colón think that he called them Indies because of East India, thinking that when he discovered the Indies he was looking for the island of Cipango, (Japan) which fell besides China or Cataio, (Cathay) and which motivated him to follow behind the sun rather than in the opposite direction; although many believe that there is no such island. In this manner, at the end, that is why they call them Indias.

(Author's translation)

So here we have a somewhat different version to the official picture of how Columbus came to discover 'America' or the Indies. It seems that he had all along a chart which he had already made for the sea captain or pilot who expired in his house giving him sailing directions to the 'Indias', and that he retained the name 'Indias' given by the pilot who had just sailed from there on his return from India but been blown off course somewhere off the west coast of Africa, taking him to new lands which he named after his point of departure.

Columbus was keen to follow up on this discovery and reading up on the works of the classical authors, learned of the hidden continent of the Carthaginians and the missing continent of Plato — Atlantis — which inspired him to follow a course to the West. He used incorrect figures for the size of the globe and incorrect distances travelled by Marco Polo to officially demonstrate that the East could be reached by sailing West, otherwise the correct distance from West Africa to China without the interceding continent would have been beyond the range in terms of supplies of the small caravels of his day as the learned cosmographers of his time well knew. Columbus knew to the very day how long it would take to get there, but perhaps influenced by the pilot's naming of the land as the 'Indias', persisted in his belief that he had found part of Asia.

A New World, of course, required new names for the territorial discoveries, and it is no surprise that the Spanish later chose 'New Spain' or 'New Castille' for their possessions in what Columbus had called the 'Indias'. Other countries did the very same with their New World possessions. New York is named after York in England and was formerly called New Amsterdam after Amsterdam in Holland. We could also note New Orleans named after Orleans in France, and numerous other examples including New England, named by explorer Captain John Smith in 1614. In all of these locations, no account whatsoever was taken of the original names given by the indigenous inhabitants.

After Amerigo Vespucci, the Italian adventurer and mercantile mariner, was the first to recognize the new land as a separate continent, mapmakers were influenced to re-name it America (see Fig. 2.01). In 1505 René II, Duke of Lorraine, gathered together a group of scholars at the Monastery of Saint Die des Vosges near Strasbourg to prepare a new map of the lands that had been discovered. Amongst these scholars was Martin Waldseemuller, a German geographer and cleric from Radolfzell, on the shores of Lake Constance.

It seems that Waldseemuller may have been in correspondence with Amerigo Vespucci, but in any event he had access to the French translation of the four accounts of the voyages of Vespucci, which the Duke had received from Lisbon.

The map which Martin Waldseemuller produced in 1507 was revolutionary for the time. It consisted of twelve sections that when cut out and assembled produced a globe the size of a grapefruit.

Fig. 2.01. Waldseemuller's map of 1507, the first to use the word 'America'.

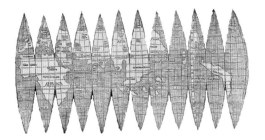

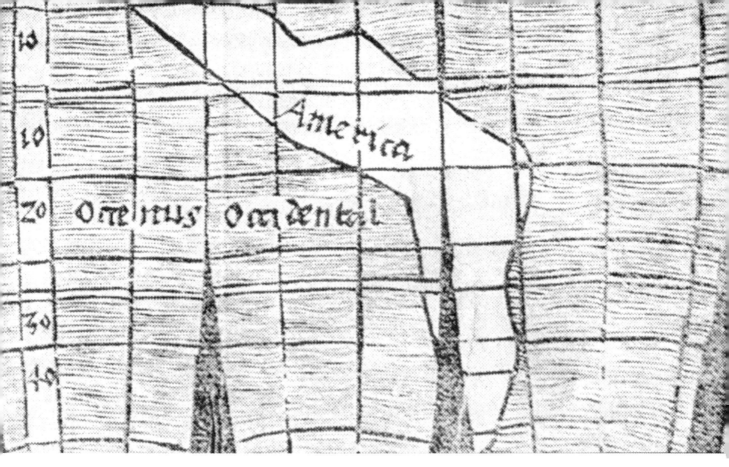

The map took twelve woodblocks to print and was drawn using
the Ptolemaic projection and titled: 'A Map of the World according
to the Tradition of Ptolemy and Amerigo Vespucci'. It was the first
map to depict the earth as a globe covering 360 degrees of longitude,
the first map to show both North and South America, the first map to
correctly pinpoint Japan and it also depicted the Pacific Ocean which
was not found until six years later by the explorer Balboa.

It was also the first map to depict the new continent which
Waldseemuller christened 'America' in recognition of the contribu-
tion made by Amerigo Vespucci in determining that it was a new
continent and not part of Asia.

The first published map to recognize America as Atlantis is that of
French cartographer Guillermo Sanson published in 1661. Based on
the work of his father, Nicolas Sanson (1600–67) Guillermo added
place names to the map of *Atlantis Insula* (Atlantis Island) which
included his interpretation of the Ten Kingdoms in South America.

Perhaps we have become so dazzled by the name America that we have become blinded to the original name of the continent, the 'Atlantis Island' being quite popular between 1665 and 1743. Or perhaps the Declaration of Independence in 1776 had something

Fig. 2.03. Waldseemuller's map showing North and South America.

Fig. 2.04. Detail from Waldseemuller's map dedicated to Amerigo Vespucci.

to do with sealing the fate of the lost continent so that the original name 'Atlantis' or 'Tahuantinsuyo' of the Incas, dropped out of sight forever.

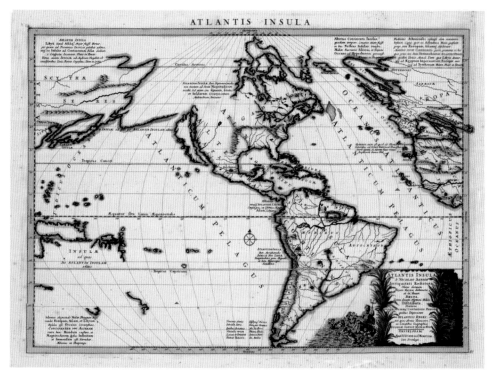

Fig. 2.05. The Atlantis Insula by Guillermo Sanson, 1661.

3. The Tomb of the Incas

Since the December 2000 expedition with the Discovery Channel to film 'Atlantis in the Andes', other new discoveries in Bolivia and Peru have come to light. For a long time it has been popular to say there were no early civilizations in America prior to, say, 1200 bc. Many people saw the similarity between American pyramids and Egyptian pyramids, but others always pointed out the dating, saying the Egyptian pyramids were truly ancient whilst the American ones were comparatively recent.

Comparing American pyramids to those in Egypt, Giza is often quoted, where the Great Pyramid of Cheops was built around 2480 bc. With a base side of 756 feet or 440 Egyptian cubits, it is a well-engineered and impressive monument, awesome in its construction and dimensions.

However, here is a little known fact. The 'Sun Pyramid' at Teotihuacan in the heart of Mexico has a base side of 738 feet — almost identical to the base of the Great Pyramid in Egypt and only 18 feet shorter per side! It is sometimes called 'the City of the Gods,' or 'where men ascended and became Gods'. Little is known about the fabulous city of Teotihuacan except that it was constructed around AD 100–200. In its day it was the sixth largest city in the world with a population of sixty to eighty thousand people, occupying an area of twenty square kilometres.

At Tucumé, in Peru, Thor Heyerdahl found the pyramids to be so massive that at first they were thought to be natural mountains. The largest of these, measuring some 1,476 × 328 × 131 ft, is rectangular in shape with its longest side almost double that of the Great Pyramid in Egypt.

Numerous other pyramids exist throughout the Americas, ranging from the beautiful temple of Kukulcan in Yucatán, to the giant adobe pyramid at Chan Chan in Peru, the pyramids of the Sun and Moon at Trujillo in Peru, dating to AD 600, and the still largely unexcavated pyramid of the Akapana at Tiwanaku in Bolivia.

All these American pyramids belong to a period much later than most of their Egyptian counterparts, but now a new discovery in Peru in the Supe valley at Caral has changed the picture. These pyramids and the city date to 2627 bc, making them older than Cheops' pyramid so we could say the pyramids at Caral are older than, or at least contemporary with, the oldest Egyptian pyramids, such as the stepped pyramid at Saqqara, south of Cairo.

Talking of pyramids reminds one of mummies, and one naturally thinks of Egyptian mummies as being the oldest and most famous in the world. However great publicity has recently been give to the Chinchorro mummies from the region between Ilo in southern Peru, and Arica, and as far south along the coast as the river Loa now in Chile. These mummies date to around 8000 BC (Sánchez and Campo 2001), making them four thousand years older than the Egyptian mummies. Workmen excavating in this area found these Inca mummies by accident, which have now been removed to the museum at San Miguel de Azapa — where incidentally, red and black pottery in the style of Quillacas on the Altiplano has also been found.

They confirm the statement by Mme Blavatsky, who visited the area in 1850, that at the base of a large rock at Arica were to be found the tombs of the Incas — a rock which she said held the key in hieroglyphics to the entrance to the legendary Inca tunnel system running through the mountains. This tunnel system is said to have run the length of the Andes and to have contained not only the accumulated wealth of the Incas and the races before them, but also, written on gold plates, the whole history of ancient South America.

But I must tell Mme Blavatsky's fascinating story in more detail, for the light that it sheds on ancient South America and the possibility of locating the tunnel entrances. Some time ago fate brought me to a building belonging to the Theosophical Society where I was able to have access to its library. I cast my eyes over the shelves of obscure books, looking for something to catch my interest. I found it in a corner, in a glass-fronted bookcase: a thick tome called *Isis Unveiled*. While the book was mostly full of obscure and hard to follow texts, one section however caught my attention and I read as follows:

> Going southward from Lima, by water, we reached
> a point near Arica at sunset, and were struck by the
> appearance of an enormous rock, nearly perpendicu-
> lar; which stood in mournful solitude on the shore,
> apart from the range of the Andes. It was the tomb of
> the Incas. As the last rays of the setting sun strike the
> face of the rock, one can make out, with an ordinary
> opera-glass, some curious hieroglyphics inscribed on
> the volcanic surface.

When Cusco *[sic]* was the capital of Peru, it contained a temple of the sun, famed far and near for its magnificence. It was roofed with thick plates of gold, and the walls were covered with the same precious metal; the eave-troughs were also of solid gold. In the west wall the architects had contrived an aperture in such a way that when the sunbeams reached it, it focussed them inside the building. Stretching like a golden chain from one sparkling point to another, they encircled the walls, illuminating the grim idols, and disclosing certain mystic signs at other times invisible. It was only by understanding these hieroglyphics — identical with those which may be seen to this day on the tomb of the Incas — that one could learn the secret of the tunnel and its approaches. Among the latter was one in the neighbourhood of Cusco, now masked beyond discovery. This leads directly into an immense tunnel which runs from Cusco to Lima, and then turning southward, extends into Bolivia. At a certain point it is intersected by a royal tomb. Inside this sepulchral chamber are cunningly arranged two doors; or, rather, two enormous slabs which turn upon pivots, and close so tightly as to be only indistinguishable from the other portions of the sculptured walls by the secret signs, whose key is in the possession of the faithful custodians. One of these turning slabs covers the southern mouth of the Liman tunnel — the other, the northern one of the Bolivian corridor. The latter, running southward, passes through Trapaca and Cobijo, for Arica is not far away from the little river called Pay'quina, which is the boundary between Peru and Bolivia.

Not far from this spot stand three separate peaks which form a curious triangle; they are included in the chain of the Andes. According to tradition the only practicable entrance to the corridor leading northward is in one of these peaks; but without the secret of its landmarks, a regiment of Titans might rend the rocks in vain in the attempt to find it. But even were someone to gain an entrance and find his way as far as the turning slab in the wall of the sepulchre, and attempt to blast it out, the superincumbent rocks are so disposed as to bury the tomb, its treasures, and — as the mysterious Peruvian expressed to us — 'a thousand warriors' in one common ruin. There is no other access to the Arica chamber but through the door in the mountain near Pay'quina. Along the entire length of the corridor, from Bolivia to Lima and Cusco, are smaller hiding places filled with treasures of gold and precious stone, the accumulations of many generations of Incas, the aggregate value of which is incalculable'.

The above lines sound like the opening plot of an Indiana Jones movie complete with secret hieroglyphic characters visible only at sunset, incalculable treasures of gold and gems and concealed tunnel entrances booby trapped to catch the unwary. Yet the 'plot' comes not from the latest Hollywood writer/producer (although it would make a good film!) but from the pen of the mysterious Mme Helena Petrova Blavatsky toiling by candlelight to study and collect all the 'lost knowledge' of the world, and presented in her mammoth book *Isis Unveiled* first published in 1877 and reprinted in New York in 1910 by the Theosophical Society of which she was principally the founder.

H.P. Blavatsky was the daughter of a Russian princess or so the introduction to her book tells us, and took her name from the army colonel she married, although she separated soon afterwards and

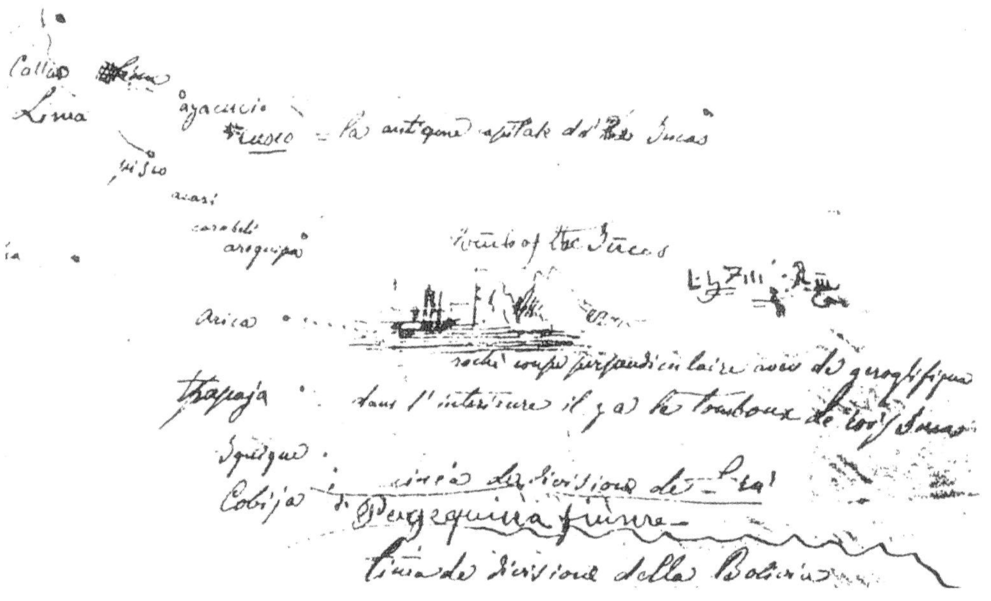

Fig. 3.01. Mme Blavatsky's Treasure Map shows the steamer arriving at Arica and the big rock known as 'The Tomb of the Incas.'

devoted the rest of her life to travelling the world and searching out lost secrets, her ultimate work being *The Secret Doctrine* published in several volumes.

We may presume Mme Blavatsky was sufficiently well connected to meet 'the right people' when she visited Peru in 1850, the tunnel legends being in vogue at that time with tales of people being lost in the catacombs beneath Lima and re-emerging days later from behind church altars until all entrances were closed on the orders of the then government.

So H.P. Blavatsky could conceivably have met the gentleman she quotes earlier in the book, who, she says, revealed to her the tunnel details, and she could conceivably have carried out the voyage where she claims to have seen the stone known as the 'Tomb of the Incas'.

Harold Wilkins (also a Theosophist) produced an imaginary map of the tunnel system (Wilkins 1946), based on Blavatsky's account. He incorrectly places the rock on the shore at Ilo and the Tomb of the Incas in the mountains just north of there, where an old map shows a village called Payquina. This was largely because he was unable to figure out the location of the river which Blavatsky called 'payquina' where she said was situated the triangle of mountains containing the entrance to the tunnel through the mountains containing the Inca Treasure.

But 'payquina' is merely a corruption for the Spanish 'pequeña' meaning 'small' and the triangle of mountains exists exactly where she said it was — down by the river Loa which was formerly the border between Peru and Bolivia in the times she was writing.

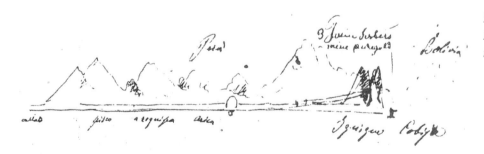

Fig. 3.02. Mme Blavatsky's sketch of the tunnel system.

Yet there are flaws in Mme Blavatsky's story. The principal discrepancy lies in the description of the border between Peru/Bolivia as being 'the river Pay'quina with Arica nearby'. The republic of

Bolivia was founded in 1825 and at that time it had an outlet to the sea with a coastline extending from the then border with Peru at the River Loa 21° 26´ S for a distance of some 325 miles to approximately 26° S in what is now Chile. Bolivia lost its western outlet to the sea as a result of the Pacific War of 1879, when Chile overran the Bolivian and Peruvian defences to extend its northern Pacific coastline as far as its present boundary with Peru just north of Arica at 18° 20´ S.

So in 1850, when Blavatsky visited Peru, the town of Arica lay in Peruvian territory, some 220 miles north of the Peru/Bolivia border which was the River Loa and not a River Pay'quina. An additional error lies in a footnote where she claims that the River Pay'quina carries specks of gold from Brazil — on the other side of the continent! It seems more likely though, that the river might simply have been described in Spanish as *pequeña*, meaning small.

So is there any truth in Blavatsky's story? Did she really get details of the tunnels from a 'gentleman in Lima'? Did she then invent a fanciful account of a voyage she never really made?

As we have seen, Harold Wilkins later produced a wonderful but imaginary map of the tunnel system, but there is no triangle of mountains near the area where he located the tomb of the Incas at Ilo. But if we disregard Wilkin's map and start again, sailing down the coast from Lima we come to Arica where the big rock stood on the shore which Blavatsky called 'The Tomb of the Incas'. This big rock or headland would have been a wonderful landmark for mariners at sea and today is called "El Morro de Arica". It marks the seaward end of a corridor running down from the Altiplano, and Arica is said to have been a seaport for the ancient Uru peoples of the Altiplano. Heading eastwards from Arica, which is one of the access routes to the Altiplano, we come to the edge of the high level plain and here, eighty miles east of Arica, there is indeed a 'curious triangle' of mountains. This group of three mountains forms a perfect right-angled triangle, not only that but it is virtually an isosceles triangle where the northern and western sides are equal.

Now to a race of master-surveyors, builders of stone cities, canals and roads spanning thousands of miles, such a perfect triangle of mountains would surely be an irresistible landmark for a tunnel entrance. Especially when one also learns that the eastern peak of the three is Nevado Sajama — the highest peak in Bolivia and itself a beacon for miles around. The southern peak is called Quimsachata and the north-west peak is a twin peak known as the *Payachatas,* or 'Guardians' — guardians of Sajama? Or of the Inca treasure?

Today the region around Sajama is designated as a national park. It is a favourite haunt of climbers and the whole region is one of outstanding natural beauty, protected by its own remoteness and inaccessibility. Indeed, local legends do talk of an entrance to the tunnel system near Sajama, but the triangle of mountains mentioned by Blavatsky was said to be further south near the river Loa.

Fig. 3.03. El Morro de Arica, or Tomb of the Incas, as it appeared around 1930.

As mentioned above, in Arica itself we can still see today the giant rock known as 'El Morro de Arica' which local legend says contains mysterious tunnels. It was at the base of this rock that numerous ancient mummies were recovered, recently carbon dated to 8000 bc, that is, four thousand years *older* than the Egyptian mummies.

It seems that, on this point at least, Blavatsky was correct, since she said at the base of the rock were to be found the tombs of the Incas. There are said to have been numerous entrances to the tunnel system, now lost, but including at the fortress of Sacsahuaman near Cuzco, the mysterious Inca site of Samaipata to the east of the Altiplano, the Island of the Sun in Lake Titicaca (said to be the birthplace of the Incas themselves), at Tiwanaku where there was said also to be a subterranean city, at Sajama, and finally the hitherto unknown triangle of mountains mentioned by Blavatsky down by the old border and the Río Loa.

If we proceed south in the direction she indicated, the river Loa itself would have been another access route which could be followed leading to the south-west corner of the Altiplano. This site up to now has seemed somewhat elusive, but its location is more *logical* than that which we would arrive at by pure guesswork. Follow the Río Loa upstream and it has its source in a triangle of mountains containing the highest peak in the south-west corner of the Altiplano — Cerro Aucanquilcha. Just as the high volcano Sajama marked the

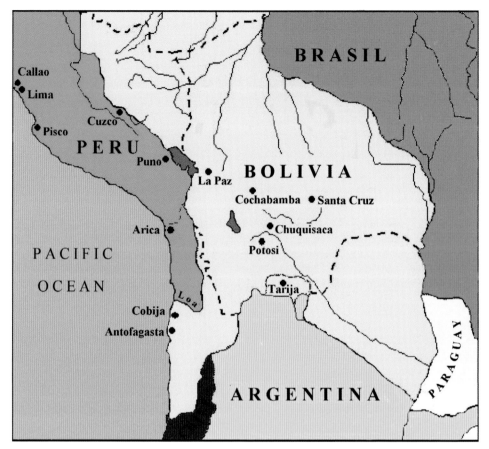

Fig. 3.04. Map showing the original boundary between Peru and Bolivia by the Río Loa, and Bolivia's coastline when the present state of Bolivia was founded in 1825.

access route (overland) to the sea from the north-west corner of the rectangular Altiplano, Aucanquilcha marks the access route from the south-west corner of the Altiplano, still used today by the railway which runs nearby and for a short distance travels alongside the river Loa and down into Chile. Bordering on the Salar de Ascotan, these mountains contain modern mining operations centred around a peak known as *Los Tres Monos* — 'the Three Monkeys'.

On the death of the last Inca emperor Atahualpa at the hands of the Spanish *conquistadores,* the Inca queen gave orders for the tunnel entrances to be sealed forever, before she herself committed suicide. Numerous pack trains of gold and jewels were hastily concealed, some thrown into lakes, like the great gold chain which disappeared forever. Some were sealed up in the tunnel system to be lost forever.

Perhaps the *Tres Monos* watch over the tunnel entrance, keeping their well known motto: 'See no evil, speak no evil, hear no evil'.

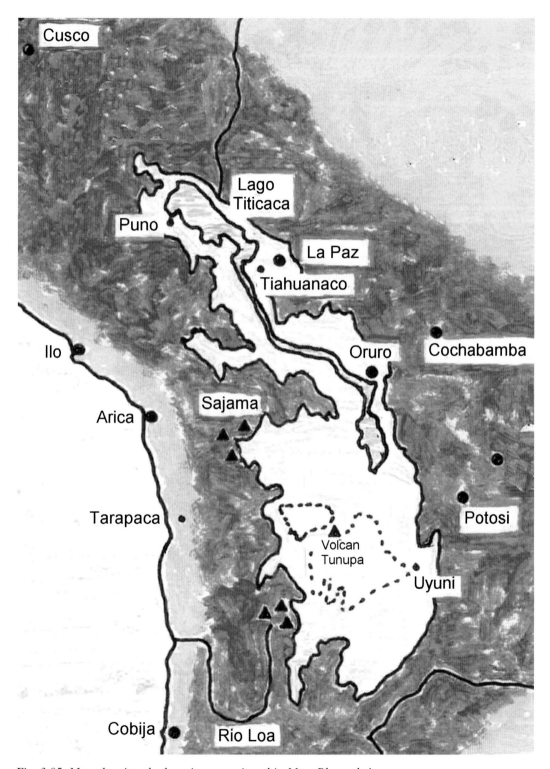

Fig. 3.05. Map showing the locations mentioned in Mme Blavatsky's treasure map.

4. History and Legends of the Incas

We have already mentioned Tunupa as the Aymara god of the sea, water, lakes and rivers and the 'Bolivian' equivalent of Poseidon, the Greek god of the sea.

We should mention also the Inca or Quechua name for this deity which was originally *Pachacamac*, Creator of the Universe, 'earth maker' originally from the Yungas region of the Andes, also known as *Viracocha* or Wiracocha in Quechua — like Poseidon the god of the seas, metallurgist, a friend, teacher and benefactor of humankind.

Just as in Greek mythology the god of the sky hurling thunderbolts was Zeus, in Andean mythology — in the version of the 'Legend of the Desaguadero' published by the University of La Paz — this position was occupied by Kon, god of wind and rain, also known as Kjuni. Tunupa or Pachacamac walks amongst the people to try and dissuade them from their evil ways and it is Kon or Kjuni who punishes them and destroys their city just like Zeus in the Atlantis legend. He is said to have destroyed a race of giants in a great flood before mankind existed.

But then Viracocha is also said to have *destroyed a race of giants in a great flood before humankind existed.*

When it comes to the Andean pantheon the picture is somewhat confusing due to the differing names for the same deities and the versions that existed at different epochs and in different places. It is difficult therefore to give a definitive version but the following account, from *History of the Incas* written by Spanish historian Pedro Sarmiento de Gamboa and translated by Sir Clements Markham of Cambridge is fascinating in itself:

> The natives of this land affirm that in the beginning, and before this world was created, there was a being called Viracocha. He created a dark world without sun, moon or stars. Owing to this creation he was named Viracocha Pachayachachi, which means 'Creator of all things'. And when he had created the world he formed a race of giants of disproportioned greatness painted and sculptured, to see whether it would be well to make real men of that size. He then created men in his likeness as they are now; and they lived in darkness ...

Viracocha ordered these people that they should live without quarrelling, and that they should know and serve him. He gave them a certain precept which they were to observe on pain of being confounded if they should break it. They kept this precept for some time, but it is not mentioned what it was. But as there arose among them the vices of pride and covetousness, they transgressed the precept of Viracocha Pachayachachi and falling, through this sin, under his indignation, he confounded and cursed them. Then some were turned into stones, others into other things, some were swallowed up by the earth, others by the sea, and over all there came a general flood which they call *uñu pachacuti,* which means 'water that overturns the land'. They say that it rained sixty days and nights, that it drowned all created things, and that there alone remained some vestiges of those who were turned into stones, as a memorial of the event, and as an example to posterity, in the edifices of Pucara, which are sixty leagues from Cuzco.

Some of the nations, besides the Cuzcos, also say that a few were saved from this flood to leave descendants for a future age. Each nation has its special fable which is told by its people, of how their first ancestors were saved from the waters of the deluge.

They say that in the time of the deluge called *uñu pachacuti* there was a mountain named Guasano in the province of Quito and near a town called Tumipampa. The natives still point it out. Up this mountain went two of the Cañaris named Ataorupagui and Cusicayo. As the waters increased the mountain kept rising and keeping above them in such a way that it was never covered by the waters of the flood. In this way the two Cañaris escaped. These two, who were brothers, when the waters abated after the flood, began to sow. One day when they had been at work, on returning to their hut, they found in it some small loaves of bread, and a jar of chicha, which is the beverage used in this country in place of wine, made of boiled maize. They did not know who had brought it, but they gave thanks to the Creator, eating and drinking of that provision. Next day the same thing happened. As they marvelled at this mystery, they were anxious to find out who brought the meals. So one day they hid themselves, to spy out the bringers of their food. While they were watching they saw two Cañari women preparing the victuals and putting them in the accustomed place. When about to depart the men tried to seize them, but they evaded their would-be captors and escaped. The Cañaris, seeing the mistake they had made in molesting those who had done them so much good, became sad and prayed to Viracocha for pardon for their sins, entreating him to let the women come back and give them the accustomed meals. The Creator granted their petition. The women came back and said to the Cañaris — 'The Creator has thought it well that we should return to you, lest you should die of hunger'. They brought them food. Then there was friendship between the women and the Cañari brothers, and one of the Cañari brothers had connexion with one of the women. Then, as the elder brother was drowned in a lake which was near, the survivor married one of the women, and had the other as a concubine. By them he had ten sons who formed two lineages of five each, and increasing in numbers they called one Hanansaya which is the same as to say the upper party, and the other Hurinsaya, or the lower party. From these all the Cañaris that now exist are descended.

In the same way the other nations have fables of how some of their people were saved, from whom they trace their origin and descent. But the Incas and most of those of Cuzco, those among them who are believed to know most, do not say that anyone escaped from the flood, but that Viracocha began to create men afresh, as will be related further on. One thing is believed among all the nations of these parts, for they all speak generally and as well known of the general flood which they call *uñu pachacuti*. From this we may clearly understand that if, in these parts they have a tradition of the great flood, this great mass of the floating islands which they afterwards

called the Atlanticas, and now the Indies of Castille,
or America, must have begun to receive a population immediately after the flood ... (Gamboa, trans.
Markham 1907, pp. 22–59)

So the salient feature of this creation myth relevant to our story
is that it names Viracocha as the creator of all things who created
a race of giants at a time when there was no sun or moon. Then
because the first people would not amend their ways being guilty
of 'pride and covetousness', Viracocha destroyed them in a flood,
the *uñu pachacuti,* or 'water that overturns the land'.

It then goes on to describe the creation of a second race of men
who became the present inhabitants and the creation of the sun and
moon while Viracocha is the great teacher who wandered throughout South America until he finally disappears into the sunset over
the ocean to the west.

But here is an interesting detail. After the flood there emerges
a survivor who ends up with a wife and a concubine from both of
whom he has *ten sons who form two lineages of five each.* Plato said
that in Atlantis the first kings were born in pairs.

He also begat and brought up five pairs of twin
male children; and dividing the island of Atlantis
into ten portions, he gave to the first-born of the
eldest pair his mother's dwelling and the surrounding allotment, which was the largest and best, and
made him king over the rest; the others he made
princes, and gave them rule over many men, and a
large territory. And he named them all; the eldest,
who was the first king, he named Atlas, and after
him the whole island and the ocean were called
Atlantic. (*Critias*, 114A)

How many 'coincidences' does it take before people realize that
these are not mere 'coincidences' but the origins of Plato's story. It
would be impossible for Plato to invent by chance, along with all
the other geographic details, the specific details like orichalcum and
the ten sons of Poseidon born in pairs, elements which are found
right here in the Andes.

In the above version, it is Taguapaca, one of the rebellious serv-
ants of Viracocha who is tied and bound then cast adrift on a balsa
in Lake Titicaca to be carried down the river Desaguadero, and

Taguapaca, or Tunupa as we otherwise know him, makes a come-back, claiming to be Viracocha himself.

Another version talks of the Inca Manco Capac carrying a gold staff and leading ten ayllu (tribal or political units or clans) from the region of Lake Titicaca to Cuzco where testing the soil by plunging the staff into the ground, he henceforth carried out his foundation of the Inca empire. Again, like Plato's Atlantis, founded with ten *lineages.*

Returning to the story of Viracocha, also formerly called *Kon-Tiki,* researchers such as Maria Rostworowski have identified four beings called 'Viracocha'. These are:

— Viracocha I, sometimes called *Pachayachachi*
    (Maker of All Things). Representing wisdom and
    world order, he is also associated with the creation
    of water and navigation techniques. 'Cocha' derives
    from the Quechua word *qucha* meaning lake or sea,
    and Viracocha is said to mean 'spume of the sea'
    so it would surely be fair for the Greeks to translate
    Viracocha as *Poseidon.* In one legend his wife was
    Mama Cocha, the 'sea mother' and patroness of sail-
    ors and fishermen, mother of Inti and Mama Quilla.
— Viracocha II, *Imaymana Viracocha,* is associated with
    plants' medicinal properties as well as agricultural
    labour.
— Viracocha III, *Tocapo,* is seen as connected with textiles.
— Finally, Viracocha IV, *Taguapaca* or *Tunupa* is
    seen as responsible for the propagation of ocean
    beings, but he is also linked with disobedience and
    rebelliousness.
    (For background see References and Sources.)

In the second version of the origins of Viracocha, he is said to have emerged from the waters of Lake Titicaca after a period of storms and floods when the earth was plunged into darkness and humankind nearly destroyed. He then went to the Island of the Sun from where he created the sun, moon and stars before continuing to Tiwanaku where he fashioned men from stone and sent them off into the four corners of the world to re-populate the world.

But in the earlier version of the origins of Viracocha, after the flood he saves two people of whom one dies and the other goes on to have ten sons in two lineages so we have not only the original five pairs of twin sons mentioned earlier, but in the subsequent legend of the origins of the Incas we have also four pairs of brother-sisters or twin offspring. As Plato said, they were *born in pairs.*

Sarmiento de Gamboa and the Atlantic Island

Pedro Sarmiento de Gamboa (1532–92) author of the preceding *History of the Incas,* is equally as colourful a character as the myths he reproduces. Considered one of the most outstanding personalities of the Spanish sixteenth century, he was a navigator, cosmographer, mathematician, soldier, historian and scholar of classical languages well versed in Plato's Atlantis which he mentions in detail in his account of the history of the Incas.

In 1555 he arrived in America where he was subjected to the Inquisition on account of his scientific and astrological activities. In 1567 he discovered the Solomon Islands, an archipelago in the Western Pacific. In 1569 he was ordered by Don Francisco de Toledo, Viceroy of Peru to write a compendium of the customs, daily life and political organization of the Incas which became his *History of the Incas* and which was sent to Philip II of Spain from Cuzco in 1572.

He fortified the Strait of Magellan as a defence against Francis Drake, founded two cities, was captured by the English on his way home to Spain, ransomed then recaptured by Huguenots and finally disappeared with the squadron carrying him to New Spain.

Pedro Sarmiento de Gamboa considered the world to be divided into five parts. The first three parts were the three continents: Asia, Africa and Europe. The fourth part was Catigara, an 'extensive land in the Indian Ocean now distinct from Asia being separated by the Strait of Malacca'. The fifth part was called 'The Atlantic Island' which exceeded all the others and 'is the land of these western Indies of Castile'.

He goes on to mention the name of the continent as 'the floating islands which they afterwards called the *Atlanticas,** and now the Western Indies of Castile or *America',* bearing in mind that he is writing shortly after the 'discovery' or rediscovery of the great continent and the name 'America' was not then as firmly established as it is today.

It is clear that he thought of Atlantis as a continent beginning immediately to the west of Spain and which continued west and included what is now South America, with the sunken part being

*Spelled as Atlanticus by Gamboa.

between Brazil and Cadiz. He deduced this based upon the statement that Atlantis was 'larger than Africa and Asia combined' so he figured Atlantis measured 2,300 leagues in width. Subtracting 1,000 leagues for the distance from Cadiz to Brazil, he concluded that Atlantis 'includes from Brazil to the South Sea which is today called America'.

So his account of the history of the Incas begins with a history and substantial overview of Atlantis, or the 'Atlanticas', which he considers to be the original name of the continent lately called America and on which the Incas are located.

As a mathematician, astrologer and navigator who was also a scholar of classical languages, he had a clear idea of when the missing part of Atlantis disappeared:

> *... debió suceder en el tiempo que Aod gobernaba el pueblo de Israel 1320 años antes de Cristo. Según todas las crónicas Solón fué en el tiempo de el rey Tarquinio Prisco de Roma, siendo Josias rey de Israel o Jerusalén, antes de Cristo 610 años. Y desde esta plática hasta que los Atlánticos habían puesto cerco sobre los Atenienses, habían pasado 9000 años lunares, que referidos a los solares suman 869 años. Y todo junto es la suma dicha arriba.*

> ... when Aod governed Israel in 1320 BC ... According to all the chronicles Solon lived in the time of King Tarquinius Priscus, King of Rome, Josiah being King of Israel at Jerusalem in 610 bc. And from this period to the time when the Atlanteans put the blockade upon the Athenians was 9,000 lunar years, which referring to solar years comes to 869 years. And both added together is the aforementioned date.

In other words, Pedro Sarmiento de Gamboa specifically spells out 1320 BC as the date for the end of Atlantis using a calendar of lunar months. I am completely surprised that of all the many investigators and academics who have studied the subject, none to my knowledge has picked up on this before. In fact, Gamboa does not even discuss the possibility that Plato might really mean nine thousand *solar* years since it is so obvious to him that *lunar* years are intended, and I think it is important to give him credit as an astronomer and classical historian who, living in the Renaissance age, knew the difference between solar and lunar years and what was intended in Plato's text.

Sarmiento de Gamboa was also of the opinion that:

> Ulysses after Troy sailed West to Portugal then to the West Indies, Yucatan and Campeche, the territory of New Spain leaving vestiges of Greek culture in clothing and vocabulary. Therefore the territories of New Spain were first colonized by Greeks, those of Catigara by Jews, while those of the rich and powerful kingdoms of Peru were colonized by Atlanteans who themselves first of all came from Mesopotamian or Chaldea, populators of the World.

This later interpretation of the origins of the people of Peru being from Atlantis is also based upon his deduction that 'South America' and 'Atlantis' were one continuous island.

Sarmiento de Gamboa took great pains to record as faithfully as possible the original stories given to him by the indigenous people and noted how the Incas themselves had a tradition of oral historians whose job it was to faithfully remember their histories as well as some painted records which were kept in a sacred temple in Cuzco, the Poquencancha.

We must remember though his motivation. In the time of Emperor Charles V, some doubt was cast on the Spanish titles to these lands since it was considered the Inca 'were and are the true and natural lords of this kingdom of Peru'.

It seems Sarmiento de Gamboa sought to justify for Philip II the acquisition of these conquered lands, and he views the Inca rulers as upstart tyrants who seized the valley of Cuzco and all the rest of the territory from Quito to Chile by force of arms, making themselves Inca overlords without the consent or election of the natives. Moreover, the fact that the Inca indulged in human sacrifices, in Sarmiento de Gamboa's eyes gave the Spanish an indisputable right to the territories, bearing in mind also the theological issues of the time and whether in Spanish eyes, natives had any rights at all.

But considering that Sarmiento de Gamboa also defined America as Atlantis, it may seem strange that his book ever got published at all. In fact the original manuscript was lost and its existence only known about through examination of correspondence between Sarmiento de Gamboa and Philip II.

An inventory of all manuscripts existing in public libraries was ordered by the German government at the end of the nineteenth century and the original manuscript was rediscovered in the University of Göttingen (Germany) in 1893 and first published in 1906.

The Aymara kingdoms

At the time of the Spanish Conquest, the Aymara kingdoms of the Altiplano still existed in pairs, the whole region was divided into Urcusuyu (of the mountains) on the one hand and Umasuyu (of the waters) on the other hand.

Herbert S. Klein gives the following account in his book *Bolivia:*

> The Aymara kingdoms characterize the later pre-hispanic period of Bolivian history. The lakeside towns along the shore of Titicaca were replaced by fortified hilltop communities and a more intensive cameloid herding culture.
>
> The somewhat aggressive Aymara-speaking peoples consisted at least seven 'nations' and each nation was divided into two separate kingdoms. Each had an *Urcusuyu* and an *Umasuyu* government, Urcusuyu being along the west and coastal regions while Umasuyu consisted of the regions along the eastern ranges and valleys.
>
> These kingdoms extended from north of Lake Titicaca along the Altiplano as far as to the south of Lake Poopó with the most powerful kingdoms centred on Lake Titicaca. (Klein 1991)

Klein goes on to say:

> It appears as if each nation was divided into two separate kingdoms. Thus the Lupaca and the Colla, to mention just the largest of these nations, both had an *Urcusuyu* and *Umasuyu* government, each with its own separate 'king' and each controlling different territories.

We can see from the map that certain of the kingdoms existed in pairs. That is to say, they were 'twin' kingdoms, just as Plato told us the Atlantis nation was ruled by five pairs of twins each with his own kingdom. Here we find that, in the last years before the Conquest, the native Aymara nation was similarly divided into 'twin kingdoms', as follows:

The Aymara kingdoms:

Urcusuyu	Umasuyu
(west side of the Andes)	(east side of the Andes)
Canchis	Canchis
Canas	Canas
Collas	Collas
Pacajes	Pacajes
Lupacas	Soras
Carangas	Charcas
Quillacas	Chuis
Caracaras (Urcu)	

Both sides — Chichas

A summary

In Bolivian legend, Tunupa, god of the sea, lakes and rivers, after opening the River Desaguadero from Lake Titicaca to Lake Poopó, disappears in the waters under Lake Poopó. But in other versions from the region around Huari and Pampa Aullagas, Tunupa reappears in the form of a woman — Thunapa — and marries Azanaques, a god who lives on a hill — in fact a hill on the other side of the lake opposite Pampa Aullagas.

The story varies from village to village, but in this version, Thunapa runs away from Azanaques, briefly pauses in Quillacas where she made a little oven to cook a meal, then passing by Pampa Aullagas lay down on the mountain thus creating the circular contours you find there today.

> *Greek version*: Poseidon, god of the sea, marries a
>   woman who lives on a hill and creates a ringed,
>   defensive formation around it.
> *Bolivian version*: Tunupa, god of the sea, lakes and
>   waterways marries a person who lives on a hill and
>   lays down on the very mountain in the location Plato
>   gave, thus creating the ringed formation to be found
>   there.

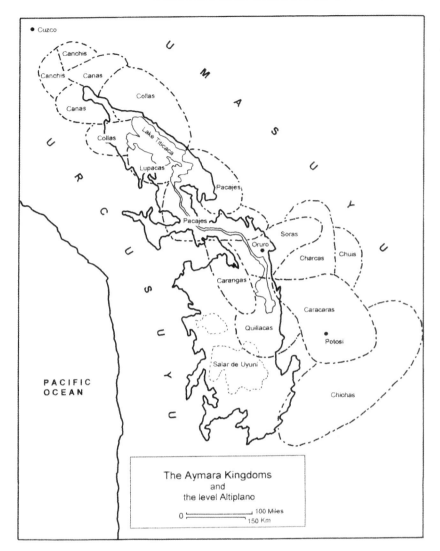

Fig. 4.01. Re-drawn by J.M. Allen from Herbert S. Klein's Bolivia.

Greek version: Poseidon had five pairs of twin sons.
Bolivian version: Virachocha had five pairs of twin sons.

Greek version: Zeus, chief of the gods, punishes the city of Atlantis and submerges it in the sea because the people no longer followed the divine laws.
Bolivian version Viracocha, chief of the gods, punishes a city for losing the divine ways and submerges it under the sea.

So can these similarities leave any doubt that the legend of Atlantis had its origins in Bolivia? After all, Plato never claimed the story of Atlantis to be a Greek invention but said it came from Egypt where it was recorded in the temples by the Egyptian priests.

Finally, it is easy to dismiss Atlantis as merely a 'coincidence' on the Altiplano, but there is one further factor regarding the site at Pampa Aullagas — from the native Aymara and Quechua, the name actually means *sunken pampa* or sunken plain, and yet another interpretation reads in Spanish *Lugar de la Sabiduría Antigua* — place of the ancient wisdom.

And Poopó, as in Lake Poopó, means 'umbilical cord' or 'where the world began'.

Fig 4.02. Pampa Aullagas or Cerro Santos Pedro Villca as the mountain is now called, formerly the site of Atlantis. Note the central island cone and surrounding low plateau as Plato called it, 'a mountain that was low on all sides'. The level plateau surrounding the main cone supported the circles of land which 'were raised a sufficient height above the level of the sea'.

5. The Aymara Language and the *Fuente Magna*

The language of the Aymara — the people who are said to have settled the shores of Lake Titicaca and occupied the Altiplano around three thousand years ago — is said to have a special quality: it is reputed to be an entirely artificial or 'man-made' language. In the early seventeenth century, the Jesuit father Ludovico Bertonio published a grammar and vocabulary of this language which he considered to be remarkably fertile and better than Spanish or Latin at handling abstract concepts. He concluded that it could not be a natural language but had to have been created artificially.

This study was developed further in 1860 by the Bolivian scholar Emeterio Villamil de Rada, in his famous book *La Lengua de Adán* ('The Language of Adam'). The work is now carried on by Bolivian researcher Iva Guzmán, an engineer and mathematician specializing in computer science who found that the logic of Aymara is trivalent compared to the bivalent logic of Spanish. That is to say, the syntax of this indigenous language is based on a non-Aristotelian logic: it has not only the two values of traditional Western logic, true or false, but three: true, false, or uncertain.

With the coming of the Inca empire, the ruling class continued to use the Aymara language, but imposed Quechua on their own subjects and conquered territories. This is said to have marked the beginning of great social problems since, although one and the same people, those who spoke one tongue could not understand the other.

During the period of the Spanish colonization, many Quechua-speaking peoples were brought to the Altiplano to work the mines there, which also altered the linguistic characteristics of the region.

We should not forget that another people lived on the Altiplano in remote times — the Uru. According to their legends, they existed before the sun at a time when the earth was dark and cold. They lived on reed islands all along the axis of the River Desaguadero from Lake Titicaca to Lake Poopó at a time when there was a wetter climate, and constructed reed boats and floating reed islands, some of which can still be seen on Lake Titicaca today. Eventually they mixed with the Aymaras and became Uru-Aymaras or in the case of the Uru-Chipayas, still live in their remote village on the edge of the Salar de Coipasa and are said to be the original builders of Tiwanaku.

During one of my stays in Bolivia, I met Bolivian journalist Manuel Rojas Boyan who had close links with the Uru and he told me that he had prepared the draft of a book proposing that the Uru were originally from Atlantis. Up to then, he had not heard of my *Atlantis; the Andes Solution* so I pointed out that he might well be right, but not a sunken Atlantis in the Atlantic, rather an Atlantis originating right here on the Altiplano.

The similarity of the Uru culture and environment to that of the Marsh Arabs in modern Iraq, or Sumerians as they were once called with their capital at Ur (alternatively called *Uru* by the French historian G. Maspero) is so striking that one wonders whether these might not only be the last remnant of the Tiwanaku builders, but of the original 'Sumerians' themselves. It is now thought that strong links exist between the Andean languages and some Asiatic languages, for example between Quechua and Turkish. Further, Bolivian anthropologist Dr Mario Montaño Aragón in his interesting book, *Semitic Roots in Aymara and Quechua Religion* (Montaño 1979), analyzes a great many words, both Quechua and Aymara, comparing them with Semitic expressions, especially Hebrew.

The Rosetta Stone of the Americas: Fuente Magna

Sometime in the year 2000, around the time of our 'Discovery' expedition, there was brought to public view a large stone bowl originally found on the shores of Lake Titicaca. It was christened the *Fuente Magna,* meaning 'great fountain' or 'great source'. Sometimes called the 'Rosetta Stone of the Americas' the object was covered inside and out in Semitic and cuneiform writing and was first found by a country peasant on an *hacienda* belonging to the Manjon family about 80 km (50 miles) north of La Paz. It was examined around 1958–60 by Bolivian archaeologist Don Max Portugal Zamora who baptized it with the name *Fuente Magna.* Its significance was not realized until later investigations revealed that the symbols appear to belong to the transitional period between ideographical writing and cuneiform, suggesting a date of 3500–3000 BC — the Sumerian/Akkadian period.

A research team returned to the original site of the finding of the dish, where a delegate from UNAAR (Unidad de Arqueología y Antropología de Bolivia) spoke to a local resident, 98-year old Maximiliano, asking if he knew anything of the bowl. At first Maximiliano couldn't remember, but when shown a picture of the

Fig. 5.01. The Fuente Magna bowl.

dish and its cuneiform writings, he recognized it straightaway and called it 'the pig's dish', mentioning that his brother had another of them, and that there were several and also pieces of pottery. (For background, see References and Sources.)

Following from this investigation, a further discovery was made on January 4, 2002, by a team including Bernardo Biadós Yacovazzo of OIIB (Omega Research Institute), and Freddy Arce Helguero of INTI (Centro de Investigación de Tecnología Integral). This new find was a monumental statue called the 'Monolith of Pokotia', similarly covered in Semitic and cunei-form symbols.

When the texts of both artefacts were analyzed by Dr Clyde A. Winters, he was of the opinion that the authors of the *Fuente Magna* bowl and Pokotia monument spoke a Sumerian language because of the appearance of both cuneiform and proto-Sumerian symbols on these figures. 'Given this visual identification of two writing systems on these artefacts, ' Winters writes, 'we have to look at Mesopotamian history and see who used both proto-Sumerian writing and who used cuneiform writing at the same time? The answer is: the Sumerians'.

Fig. 5.02. Detail of the Fuente Magna bowl.

Dr Mario Montaño Aragón, whose work we have mentioned above, has found startling linguistic evidence that indicates a Sumerian substratum in the Aymara and Quechua languages, and the Sumerian writing on the *Fuente Magna* bowl and Pokotia statue suggest that there was a Sumerian presence in ancient South America.

If this is so, the Andes could well be the source of the tin and copper supplies known to have been imported to the Middle East by the Sumerians. But we must also raise the question: did the Sumerians sail to South America? Or, conversely, did the Sumerians themselves originate in South America?

In his book *Legend — the Genesis of Civilization,* archaeologist David Rohl proposes that the ancient Egyptian culture was founded by Sumerians who landed on the shores of the Red Sea. He shows pictures of early reed ships painted on cave walls in the Eastern Egyptian Desert. What he does not mention, is that these reed ships painted on the cave walls are also identical to reed ships in Bolivia (see Rohl 1999).

Ancient civilization in South America

Up to now, the main objection to Atlantis being situated in Bolivia is that it is said that there was no civilization in Bolivia before around 1200 bc. It was also said that no writing existed in ancient South America.

However with the discovery of the pyramids of Caral, dating from 2627 bc, and now, *Fuente Magna,* a bowl inscribed with cuneiform, proto-Sumerian writing dating to 3500 bc, it can be demonstrated that there was writing in ancient South America. Could these proto-Sumerians be the missing 'Atlantean' culture the Andes Solution has been looking for?

Traces of coca, a plant of South American origin, have been found in Egyptian mummies dating to 1200 bc, and coca has also been found growing on the island of Madagascar which would have been on the sailing route from Río de la Plata to Mesopotamia. On the island of Bahrain in the Persian Gulf, Thor Heyerdahl found interlocking stones of Andean-type construction at the lower levels of walls under excavation.

It is clear that civilization in ancient South America is much older and more extensive than has been previously recognized. There are said to be over 30,000 archaeological sites in Bolivia and many of these have not been at all investigated and those that have, only partially explored. It is now acknowledged that a civilization existed throughout the whole of Amazonia where previously it was thought there was none. And in the Beni (lower Bolivia), a people lived on a flood plain on mounds connected by long straight causeways covering many miles of territory.

The dating of the *Fuente Magna* bowl pushes the origins of South American civilization back to a period contemporary with or earlier than Egyptian or Sumerian civilization, and other recent finds have not yet been published which may go still further back in time. There remains much to be uncovered or discovered and the *Fuente Magna* bowl is about to open a whole new chapter in the history of Bolivia, South America or Atlantis as it was once called, and the world. (For background on recent discoveries, see References and Sources.)

The Akakor expedition

Indeed, in August 2004, a combined Italian/Brazilian expedition named Akakor made a wonderful discovery at a depth of 120 metres (394 ft) under the waters of Lake Titicaca — the remains of ancient walls and constructions dating to 4000 bc, definitive proof that previous cultures had been drowned by the rising waters of Lake Titicaca due to climate change (for background, see References and Sources).

The recent discovery of ancient constructions submerged under Lake Titicaca is a remarkable achievement, but should it come as a surprise? After all the legends speak of ruins under the lake and the history of humankind is littered with civilizations which have come and gone, cities which have flourished and disappeared, many due to climate change or natural disasters, examples of which might be Pompeii buried by the volcano Vesuvius, Akrotiri buried under volcanic ash when the island of Thera erupted, Troy, lost through aeons of time and only remembered as a legend until located by Heinrich Schliemann, Knossos on Crete, Ur, Babylon and Nineveh. And then there are the famous cities of Sodom and Gomorrah mentioned in the Bible but swept away by earthquakes and never located.

Over the centuries, people have frequently built cities on volcanoes or valley floors subject to flooding, and the people occupying the Altiplano next to Lake Poopó were just as much at risk of being submerged under the waters of the lake as those ancient people whose constructions have now been found under the waters of Lake Titicaca.

There remains one great city or civilization known only by legend and which people continue to doubt ever existed. It is the story of a city destroyed by earthquakes and overwhelmed by a great flood, all of which took place in the space of a single day and night. The name of this city is Atlantis.

We have to remember that although Plato said the island sank into the sea, the English philosopher Sir Francis Bacon said in fact it was the rising waters of the lake which submerged the island — and isn't that just like what happened with the ruins under Lake Titicaca?

In fact all around Pampa Aullagas are underground springs, so when it rains in another part of the country, it can rapidly flood the level Altiplano. That is why the story reminds me of the story of the flood in Genesis, when the mountains 'fled away and were found no more' and God 'broke open the chains of the fountains of the deep'.

Atlantis never was a sunken continent in the middle of the Atlantic Ocean, but in reality was based upon an indigenous Andean culture. And, in the end, Atlantis was simply overwhelmed by climate change and natural disasters typical of the Altiplano.

6. Atlantis Today

Fig. 6.01. Sailing to Atlantis.

The greatest problem with Atlantis is simply this: How to recognize it on the ground if you find it! True enough we have Plato's detailed description, a mountain low on all sides in the centre of the Plain, five miles from the sea, sunk by earthquakes and submerged by the sea. And with the particular features of two rings of land and three of water surrounding the central cone.

Fig. 6.02. Ron Miller's beautiful illustration of Atlantis for his book of Jules Verne's *Twenty Thousand Leagues under the Seas.*

With these details many European artists have sought to re-construct Plato's Atlantis. With visions ranging from futuristic 'space' concepts (it has even been claimed that Atlantis was a planet!) to baroque style Venices and sunken Greek palaces as in Ron Miller's beautiful drawing for Jules Verne's *Twenty Thousand Leagues under the Seas,* as the title should correctly be translated from the French, *Vingt Mille Lieues sous les Mers.*

But we can be certain of one thing: a city which was destroyed by earthquakes to the point where, as Plato tells us, 'the site was unsearchable due to the shoal mud which the island threw up as it settled down', certainly would not look like the romantic image painted in Jules Verne's version, with divers swimming around virtually intact Greek-style temples.

We should also consider the destructive forces of earthquakes, and especially those in the great fault line of the Andes. As seismologist Mark Andrew Tinker explains:

In 1960, the largest earthquake ever recorded occurred along the Southern Chilean subduction zone. Difficult to rate on any magnitude scale (magnitude of approximately 9.5), this earthquake ruptured an area over 1000 km (620 miles) in length and 200 km (125 miles) in depth. Thus, the South America and Nazca plates moved past each other a phenomenal 24 metres (80 ft) on average for the entire area of 200,000 square kilometres (77,500 sq miles).

Although the plates slipped past each other at about 2 km/sec, (1.25 miles/sec) it took many violent minutes for the entire area to undergo slip. This single event released more energy than all the earthquakes in the entire world combined for any average 3–4 year period.

On the Altiplano, there are three sources of regional earthquakes. The first is the aforementioned interaction between South America and the Nazca plate. The second regional source of earthquakes is within the Nazca slab, which dives beneath South America and dips towards the east at a thirty degree angle to a depth in excess of 600 km (372 miles).

As it moves through the upper mantle, it is subjected to various stresses that it accommodates by brittle failure, or earthquakes. On June 9, 1994, such an event happened near La Paz, Bolivia. This event was the largest of its kind in recorded history at magnitude 8.2. It literally made the earth ring like a bell for over 48 hours. People in Canada claimed to have felt it!

The third and final source of regional earthquakes is the Altiplano itself. It possesses some of the thickest continental crust on earth at approximately 65 km (40 miles) only the upper portion of which is seismically active. (From 'Chasing Earthquakes in Bolivia', M.A. Tinker, Seismic Observatory, Department of Geosciences, University of Arizona, Tucson, US.)

Imagine these forces applied to old buildings which may have existed on the site, or their ruins, and you can see the problem of distinguishing between shattered stones which may have been part of man-made structures and those produced by natural volcanism.

We can see then that the Altiplano is in a prime earthquake zone, and with the ground 'ringing like a bell' and moving at a rate of 2 km/sec, there may not be so much left of Atlantis after all when we do find it!

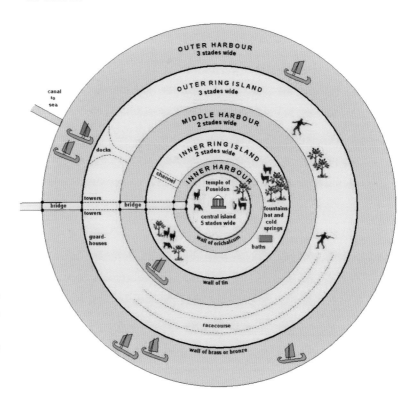

Fig. 6.03. Plan view of Atlantis showing the circular rings of land surrounding the central island. The central island is 5 stades in diameter, enclosed by a ring of water 1 stade wide, then ring of land 2 stades, ring of water 2 stades, ring of land 3 stades, ring of water 3 stades.

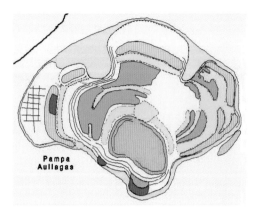

Fig. 6.04. The actual site at Pampa Aullagas showing the central island cone and the remains of rings of land and sand-filled channels.

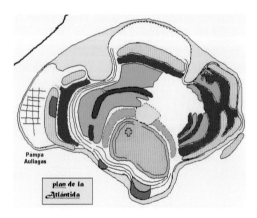

Fig. 6.05. How the site at Pampa Aullagas might look if the remaining sandy channels were filled with water.

There must have existed a time when the higher water levels of the lake would have been sufficient to penetrate the perimeter of the island entering the natural concentric depressions, thus creating concentric rings of land and sea rendering the site as Plato said, 'impassable to men for ships and sailing had not yet been invented'.

The innermost channel, coloured light blue, is today higher up the volcano so it is not clear whether this was part of the numbered circles described by Plato or whether there was another circle of water on the outside of the volcano, bearing also in mind that he did say the circles were 'carved out of the midst of the island'.

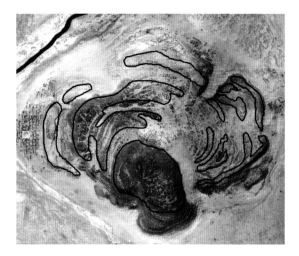

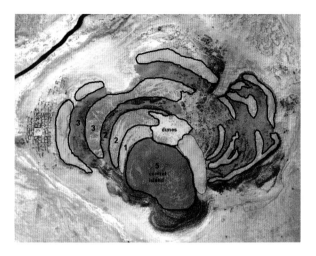

Fig. 6.06. Air photo of Pampa Aullagas with some of the rings of land outlined. In the photo above, travelling eastwards from the village of Pampa Aullagas, one comes to what at first appears to be the outer ring of land described by Plato, though subsequent study suggests that it was part of an outer ring of rock containing the outer ring of water 3 stades wide. Plato mentioned that they bored through the rock to the outermost circle of water and that the circular channels were 'carved out of the midst of the island' suggesting all the circular water channels were within the actual volcano and not on the surrounding alluvial plain. Study of the air photo suggests that this ring of land faced in rounded stones may be an artificial construction although another opinion is that it was formed by lava flow. On the inside it has been sunk by earthquakes to form a canal-like depression.

One then climbs the next inner ring before crossing the middle ring partly filled in with sand then coming to another circular depression or channel at a higher level then arriving at the central cone. The depressions on the remainder of the level plateau when filled with water would have made ideal natural harbours. Photo: Instituto Geográfico Militar, La Paz.

Fig. 6.07. The photo above, shows the actual rings of land still remaining as plotted on site by GPS and how they may appear when the sandy canals are filled with water.

The inner ring on the northern side (1), however, is quite high above the remaining island suggesting that this side of the island has risen in elevation, making it unclear whether this was actually part of Plato's scheme or there may have been another ring of water on the outside of the volcano. Or possibly it may have been part of the central cone which has collapsed partly filling the middle ring at number (2). The steep cone (5) is about 5 stades of 300 ft (92 m) in diameter at its base or 5 stades of 165 ft in diameter at its summit and the channels shown here also use smaller 'stades' of 165 ft (50.3 m) which is 100 Sumerian cubits of 19.8 inches.

Three smaller concentric rings of water are also seen on the south-east side of the site although several of the channels as they appear today may have been formed by or after the destruction by earthquakes. Indeed, it may even be possible that the complete eastern arm has been moved outwards from the centre of the volcano making it difficult today to align the rings into perfect circles.

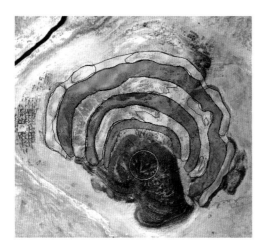

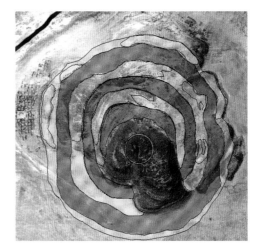

Fig. 6.08. The site appears to have suffered considerable damage from earthquakes. Some parts have sunk, others risen in elevation whilst others appear to be twisted round and even moved sideways, as if struck by a huge force from the west, north and south-west.

In the above photo, the outer ring of rock has been joined up and the eastern arm of the volcano moved closer into the centre so that the outer channels follow a continuous circle. The rings fall in the correct proportions of 1 stade of water, 2 stades of land, 2 stades of water, 3 stades of land and 3 stades of water using stades of 165ft.

The central island was reported 5 stades in diameter, shown here as at the top of the steeply sided volcanic cone. This also clears up the mystery of how it 'looked towards the south and was sheltered from the north winds' since the central island cone is of a horseshoe shape, open towards the south and sheltered by the rim of the volcano from the north.

Fig. 6.09. 'There were two rings of land, and three of water, which he turned as with a lathe, each having its circumference equidistant every way from the centre'.

It is not known whether the outer ring of rock may have continued on the southern side and subsequently disappeared, but here it is shown restored to give an idea of how the volcano may have looked before its destruction and to give a more complete, circular appearance.

According to Plato, the outermost ring was a ring of water, yet logically the outermost ring must have been a ring of land or rock in order to contain the water, such as the embankment next to the village.

The reconstructed rings of land have been mirrored to show the possible shape of the original island assuming that the complete southern section has been destroyed by the earthquakes.

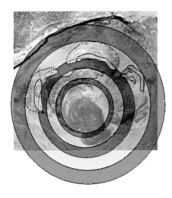

Fig. 6.10. In the wet season the water from the lake encircles the entire island. Even today, it would be possible to reconstruct the site according to the scheme of Plato. In this interpretation, the outer embankment behind the village is assumed to be the outer circle of land and parts of the central cone as seen today, are assumed to have collapsed into the innermost channel. Using stades of 300 ft, a 3 stade ring of land has been continued around the south of the site and enclosed by a 3 stade ring of water fed by the river Laca Jahuira, which represents the original canal to the sea.

The sunken northern and western 'leaves' and the remaining outer rings of land fit perfectly on the three stade wide ring of land and the remaining inner ring of land fits perfectly well on the two stade ring of land as described by Plato although it is possible that his description, being based on a natural feature, should be read as a generalization rather than looking for a perfect geometry.

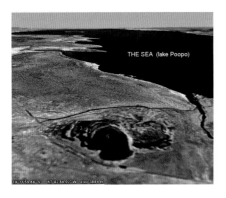

Fig. 6.11. Oblique satellite image of the site at Pampa Aullagas with the rings numbered. This satellite image shows the site at Pampa Aullagas in the dry season. Lake Poopó has receded leaving the island as a volcano on dry land, as Plato said, '50 stades from the sea'.

The island appears to consist of two volcanic events, the low plateau which Plato called 'the mountain low on all sides' and which contains the concentric circles, and the steep cone (5) which actually lies on the southern side of the low plateau.

The island is honeycombed with interior channels or vents which produce moisture and conduct water in the wet season to various parts of the island and with water emanating from the top of the volcano and a better climate, the whole site may also be reminiscent of the 'hanging gardens of Babylon'...

Fig. 6.12. Typical imaginary drawing of Atlantis showing the concept of the concentric rings of land and sea.

Fig. 6.13. The outer channel circles to the left.

Fig. 6.14. View inside inner channel on the north-west looking left.

Fig. 6.15. The outer channel continues to the right then disappears into thin air.

Fig. 6.16. Inner channel on the northern side.

Fig. 6.17. View inside inner channel on the north-west side.

As to the perfectly circular canals we had imagined based on popular drawings, I looked up Plato's words again and in his opening description of Atlantis he says: '... Near the plain at a distance of 50 stades (from the sea) there stood a mountain that was low on all sides'. He goes on to say that Poseidon married a damsel called Cleito who lived on this mountain, and then:

> ... to make the hill whereon she dwelt impregnable
> he broke it off all round about; and he made circular
> belts of sea and land enclosing one another alter-
> nately, some greater, some smaller, two being of land
> and three of sea, which he carved as it were out of
> the midst of the island; and these belts were at even
> distances on all sides, so as to be impassable for man;
> for at that time neither ships nor sailing were as yet
> in existence. (*Critias,* 113D)

> (Cp. the Jowett translation: 'Poseidon ... *breaking the
> ground* enclosed the hill all round, making alternate
> zones of sea and land larger and smaller, encircling
> one another'.)

And that was what we found, except that the sea had dropped and the 'zones of sea' were now sandy-bottomed depressions or channels, but it was not difficult to imagine them having been filled with water at some earlier date.

The standard tourist route had evolved by people climbing the stone-faced outer ring behind the village, then down into the outer canal, then up a broad embankment before descending a broad inner channel at a higher level probably formed after the collapse of the central island, then the remains of the central cone itself. The descent was by a different route on the same side of the volcano and passing through what was probably the original inner channel.

It was not until October 2005 when, late one Sunday evening after already climbing all over the volcano, I had the chance to visit the south-east side of the plateau surrounding the central cone.

Beginning at the outer rim we crossed a broad depression or channel, the vegetation on the floor showing signs of moisture. Then a ring of land and another concentric circular channel. Another ring of land and an inner circular channel.

The rings of land were covered in sharp-pointed *katawi* or fossilized lake sediments and, taken together, conformed perfectly well to Plato's account of the three rings of water separated by two rings of land although some of the depressions as they exist today may have been formed by the earthquakes which sunk the island.

At the time when filled by water from the nearby lake, they would have formed perfect natural harbours, and to the Uru, *the men of water*, the whole complex must have formed an irrestible natural port and fortress. At a time when people lived on the mountains because the lower Altiplano was covered by water, it would be inconceivable that people would not have lived here, at a time going back to great antiquity.

Having seen these three particular channels or harbours, it is clear there is no need for a perfectly circular geometry surrounding the whole island as exists in many popular drawings following the concept of Plato, as there is no other way to describe the island but as concentric circles of land and (formerly) sea.

Restoring Plato's missing geometry conforms better to his description, but even without that certainly it is a central island surrounded by concentric rings of water and land in a natural formation, for what we have here is not the Atlantis of Hollywood or science-fiction fantasy, but the *real* Atlantis.

Fig. 6.18. Inner channel on the south-east side.

Fig. 6.19. Middle channel on the south-east side.

Fig. 6.20. Outer channel on the south-east side.

Fig. 6.21. View of the outer embankment covered in rounded stones. The lower part is devoid of stones and covered in sand suggesting the level plain has dropped in elevation leaving the original site high in the air.

Fig. 6.22. This artist's impression, 'Atlantis on the Altiplano' by Major Lee Smart — a member of the 1998 Kota Mama expedition — is remarkable in that he had never actually visited this site, and at that time neither had I, yet what he has drawn is an excellent impression of what the site actually looks like, including the two gaps seen on the outer ring which also exist on site.

7. Sinking into the Sea

At a later time there were earthquakes and floods of
extraordinary violence, and in one single dreadful day
and night the island of Atlantis was swallowed up by
the sea and vanished ... (*Timaeus*, 25D, trans. Lee)

Plato's account of the island finally sinking into the sea in the space
of a single day and night of rain and being destroyed by earthquakes
and floods is perfectly feasible on the Altiplano and indeed such a
site exists at Pampa Aullagas at the southern end of Lake Poopó,
exactly as Plato said it should be. Not only has the level plain surrounding Pampa Aullagas sunk in elevation, but many of the stones
from the wall surrounding the site have totally disappeared beneath
the ground. Part of the face of the original volcano has similarly
fallen away and a large quantity of sand covers parts of the site,
perhaps corresponding to 'the shoal mud which the island threw
up as it settled down', or — in modern terms — the fine particles
brought to the surface in a process called 'liquefaction' where the
surface turns to a mud-like substance sucking any available stones
beneath the ground.

At the time of the formerly higher lake levels, there would have
been natural inner harbours and they do enclose each other 'like
cartwheels', as Plato said, but the site as it appears today appears to
be a natural formation more in the form of a cross with a circular
island cone at its centre, circular channels surrounding it and with
the southern arm missing. But then the arms of the cross are formed
by the opening up of two great sandy bays probably caused by
earthquakes, so it seems possible that the circular channels could
have at one time run continuously round the site before the opening up of the sandy bays. Plato did mention that it was necessary to
open up an entry from the canal to the sea through the rock to the
outermost circular channel.

Given Plato's liking for the circular form, he may have
'rounded up' the form of the site to give a perfect geometry, but
the outer ring does have gaps where you could sail into the inner
harbours.

People sometimes say; 'How can Atlantis be in the Andes when
it is supposed to have sunk into the sea?' We must remember that
Atlantis according to Plato was on a level plain 'high above the

level of the sea and enclosed by mountains' and that in fact, the entire plain has been periodically submerged beneath water, that is, it became a giant inland sea at various dates going back thousands of years succeeded by dry periods. An analysis of core samples taken from the centre of the Salar de Uyuni shows that there are several layers of salt and layers of lacustrine mud, revealing that the plain was successively covered by deep lakes alternating with dry spells.

These lakes were fed by water flowing south via the Desaguadero river from Lake Titicaca in the north and in these periods the precipitation was much greater than today. Atlantis is presumed to have existed in one of the 'wet' periods when its canals were fed by the overflowing waters of Lake Titicaca.

The two most probable dates for the end of Atlantis are: (a) 11,000 bc, which is not far from the date given by Plato; or (b) 1200 bc, if we substitute 'months' for 'years'.

Going back in time, we can say with certainty that Atlantis could not have existed in the period 30,000–28,000 BC because at this time the entire Altiplano was covered by the deep paleolake Minchin.

Similarly it could not have existed at the time of the next wet spell from 23,000–13,000 BC because from 16,000–13,000 bc, the Altiplano was covered by paleolake Tauca to a depth of 459 ft.

From 11,000–9500 bc, Lake Titicaca overflowed again and during this period the central Altiplano was covered by a shallow paleolake 'Coipasa'. Atlantis could not have existed at the time of the lake itself since the paleolake would have inhibited the route of the 'perimeter canal' unless Atlantis existed before the arrival of Lake Coipasa and it was Lake Coipasa itself which drowned Atlantis in 11,000 bc. This would also be before the formation of the salt salars due to repeated flooding and drying when the ground would have comprised lacustrine mud ideal for cultivation and also the climate would have been 6° warmer.

To obtain a more complete climate record, a team of geologists led by *Science* co-author Paul A. Baker of Duke University collected new samples of the mud from Lake Titicaca at 270 feet, 450 feet and 690 feet below the surface. Baker with Robert Dunbar and their colleagues were able to reconstruct a history of precipitation in the Altiplano by determining how water levels in Lake Titicaca changed during the last 25,000 years.

After analyzing all three core samples, the scientists concluded that the lake — and therefore the entire Altiplano — has undergone a series of dramatic changes since the Ice Age was at its peak between 26,000 and 15,000 years ago. According to the *Science* study:

Fig. 7.01. The Altiplano covered by paleolake Tauca with Lake Titicaca to the north.

Lake Tauca

Pacific Ocean

Lake Titicaca was a deep, fresh and continuously overflowing lake during the last glacial stage, signifying that the Altiplano of Bolivia and Peru and much of the Amazon basin were wetter than today.

Then, about 15,000 years ago (13,000 bc), the Altiplano underwent a significant change. A dry era was launched, which continued for the next two thousand years, causing Lake Titicaca to drop significantly.

Between 13,000 and 11,500 years ago (11,000– 9500 bc), Titicaca began overflowing once again. This wet period was followed by fifteen hundred years of relative dryness, followed by another 2,500 years of heavy precipitation as the lake again rose to overflow levels.

Then, about 8,500 years ago, the lake level fell sharply as the Altiplano again became dry. But heavy precipitation would return for another one thousand years, only to be followed by an extremely dry period between six and five thousand years ago, during which Titicaca fell some 250 feet below its present-day level — its lowest level in 25,000 years. Titicaca finally began rising again 4,500 years ago. Since then, the southern portion of the lake has overflowed its banks numerous times.

The fact that alternating periods of dryness and wetness occur on a millennial time-scale or longer may be influenced, in part, by the behaviour of the Earth as it orbits the sun. For example, the Earth's rotational axis gradually changes direction every 26,000 years — a process called precession. As a result, parts of the Earth that are relatively close to the sun during summer today will be farther away during summer thousands of years from now. (Baker, Dunbar *et al.* 2000)

With the wet period beginning 2500–1900 bc, a paleolake formed in the River Desaguadero valley suggesting that at this period the water levels might have been correctly balanced to feed the canals of Atlantis. It also suggests that Lake Poopó could have formed an almost continuous sea stretching right up to Lake Titicaca.

Following a 'short' dry spell of four hundred years, the next wet spell was from 1500–1200 bc, and it seems probable that this is the date Plato referred to as the end of Atlantis since he says, 'nine thousand is the sum of years (that is, lunar years, meaning months) since the war occurred', and 1200 BC is broadly speaking concurrent with the Trojan war and the invasion of Egypt by the 'Sea Peoples' which could correspond to the war against Egypt which Plato described. Indeed, we know that major flooding occurred at that time because a recent survey by the United States Geological Survey using sidescan radar in Lake Titicaca tells us that the lake overflowed about three thousand years ago, drowning many habitations and settlements on the edge of the lake. Even in modern times, flooding is a recurring problem in this area and modern proposals are in hand to dig relief channels to combat this problem. Yet even today, it would still be possible to dig a large canal across the northern section of the Altiplano to collect the rivers which come down from the mountains and divert this water into Lake Poopó, making a return to the Salar de Coipasa by a similar canal at the southern end of the lake via Pampa Aullagas alias 'Atlantis'!

But the acid test, of course, and that which people want, is to find something on the ground which could be used as actual proof to corroborate Plato's tale. In the beginning I accepted his words that 'the city disappeared beneath the sea, and that the site was unsearchable due to the shoal mud which the island threw up as it settled down'. So I concentrated my search on finding remains of a vast canal 600 feet wide which he said circulated around the plain.

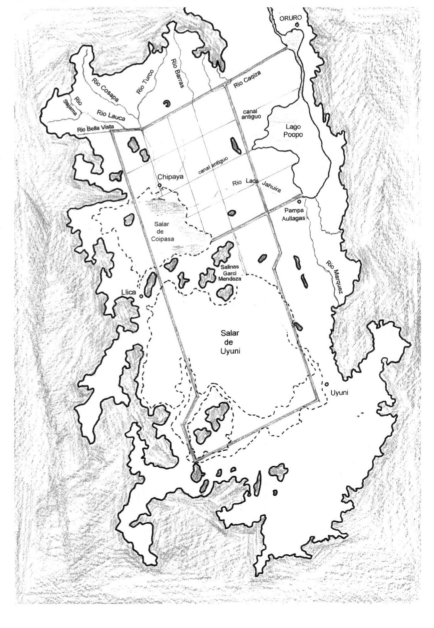

Fig. 7.02. Even today, it would be possible to reconstruct Plato's canal to prevent flooding.

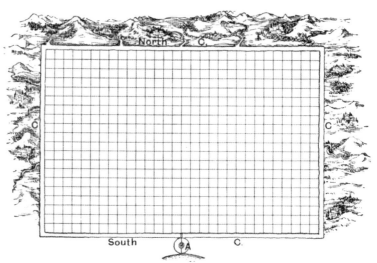

THE ISLAND OF ATLANTIS (*Critias*, 118 A ff.).—Plan of Plain, 2000 × 3000 stades, enclosed on all sides by main canal (C), 10,000 stades long, and intersected by 29 vertical and 19 horizontal cross-trenches. On all sides except the south the plain is encircled by mountains, with streams, villages, forests, etc. At its central point (A) on the south the canal is joined by the canal which runs through the city to the sea.

Frontispiece

Fig. 7.03. Textbook view of the level rectangular plain with the chequered canal system described by Plato and the city midway along the plain next to the sea.

RIGHT: Fig. 7.04. The level rectangular plain of the Altiplano with theoretical grid of canals and the site at Pampa Aullagas in the correct position where Atlantis should be, in the centre of the plain, next to the sea.

It was only years after beginning my search that I came across the book *New Atlantis* by the great English philosopher Sir Francis Bacon, who correctly identifies South America as Atlantis. Bacon says that Plato got it wrong, and the island city did not sink beneath the sea but was submerged beneath the waters of a rising sea which prevented people from returning for many years ... and the site at Pampa Aullagas does in fact tally with the picture which Bacon presented.

And where did Sir Francis Bacon get his information from? None other than Sarmiento de Gamboa who was taken prisoner onboard one of Sir Walter Raleighs's ships and subsequently presented to the English court (Coote 1993, p.103) and, in consequence, had the opportunity to meet Sir Francis Bacon.

The whole Altiplano is a delicately balanced system and just as Plato's theoretical canal could make the water flow away from the lake or towards the lake, similarly at Lake Titicaca old canals have been found which similarly carried the waters either to the lake or from the lake depending on the levels.

In the region around Lake Titicaca, old irrigation beds have been revived in the form of raised fields. The water raises the local temperature so that ground which has been abandoned for centuries is now very productive and can produce — as Plato said — 'two crops per year'.

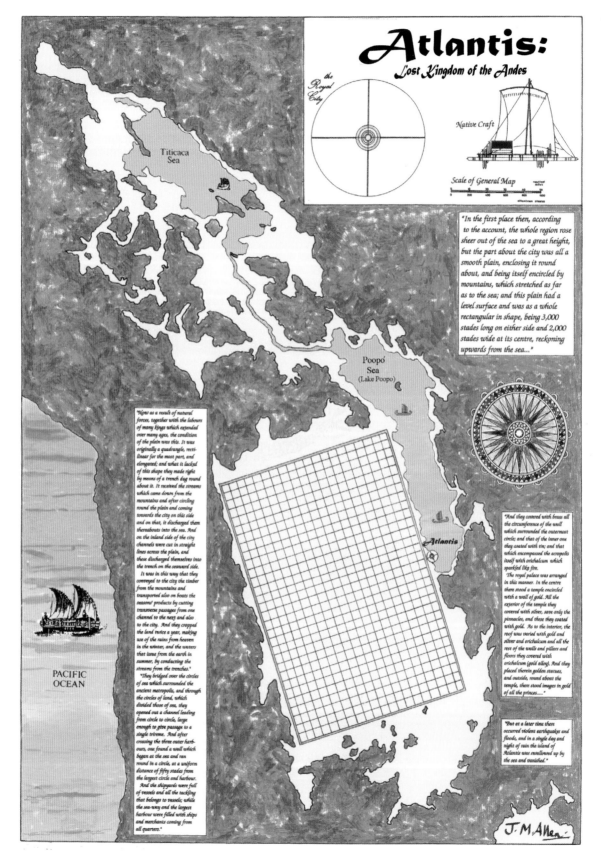

Back in the year 1983, I bought some images from Landsat. The pictures were very small scale, but even so, it seemed that remains of ancient irrigation canals could be seen on them in the area near Lake Poopó. I sent them to the RAF hoping for a confirmation but regrettably in their opinion there were no canals at all, the area was unsuitable for canals and only fault lines and trellised drainage patterns could be found.

High-resolution satellite images today tell a different story. The whole area around and to the south of Lake UruUru is covered with canals, in straight lines just as Plato said and parallel to each other, with transverse canals exactly like the generally envisaged 'chequerboard' pattern.

It is not possible to give a date for the canals purely from the satellite photos. Some appear to be very ancient and conform to

Fig. 7.05. High-resolution satellite image shows the straight canals and the transverse passages cut across the plain. 'Channels were cut in straight lines across the plain, and they transported also on boats the seasons' products, by cutting transverse passages from one channel to the next'. (Critias, 118C)

Plato's description of parallel channels. Others appear to be fairly recent and used today for irrigation and drainage.

But the region is sparsely populated. The large number of canals, many disappearing beneath the ground and no longer functioning, suggests a previously large population and the people today face the same problems of flooding and irrigation that they did in the time of Plato's Atlantis with the same solutions of canals and transverse drainage ditches.

And that's what Atlantis was, a level rectangular plain, with at its centre an island with concentric rings of land and water and on the plain itself a system of canals dug in straight lines and parallel to each other, that is — the Altiplano!

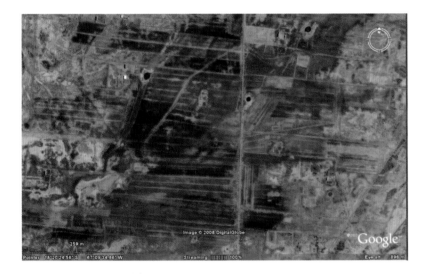

Fig. 7.06. Parallel canals with a transverse watercourse to bring water from one of the feeder wells.

Fig. 7.07. Detail from high-resolution satellite image showing parallel canals and transverse passages.

Fig. 7.08. Another system of channels connects wells drawing water from the underground water table, and appears to supply the parallel canals.

Fig. 7.09. Detail of one of the wells 200 ft in diameter and 110ft on the inside, with its interconnecting channel. One can see clearly that the underground water level is no longer high enough for the canals to function.

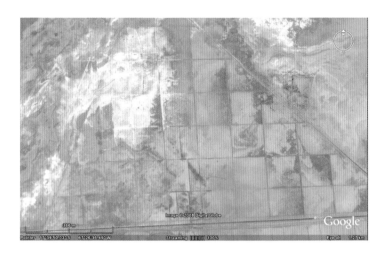

Fig. 7.10. Some of the canals form a chequered pattern.

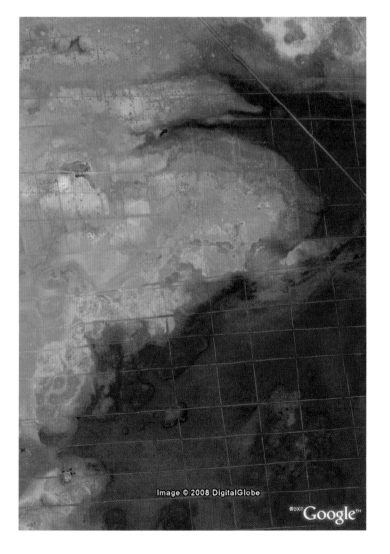

Fig. 7.11. A chequerboard pattern of canals extends into Lake UruUru (Lake Poopó). The surrounding terrain is now mostly salt desert.

8. The Circle and the Cross

People often talk of 'the Cross of Atlantis', but where that comes from, unless it is some sort of New Age vision, I do not know. I do know that Plato never mentioned it. In fact Plato was more obsessed with a perfectly circular geometry than with any cross-shaped configuration.

So his circular city is of almost perfect dimensions. Surrounding the circular central island five stades in diameter was a circular ring of water one stade in width, then a ring of land two stades in width followed by a ring of water two stades in width, followed again respectively by rings of land and water each of three stades in width.

This almost suggests that the rings of land were constructed so that the rings of water corresponded in size to the volume of land excavated and heaped up on the adjoining land. But what we have found is at this point it is difficult to separate what might have been man-made from what might have been natural.

And were the perfect circles created in the mind of Plato who, after all, wrote above the entrance to his Academy, 'Let no one ignorant of geometry enter here!'

Immediately to the east of the village of Pampa Aullagas one climbs the outer ring of land which possibly may be an artificial embankment faced in rounded stones. These stones are continuous around the whole site forming a kind of wall — consistent with the fact that Plato told us the island was surrounded with a wall of stone. But on the inside of this embankment, the terrain has been sunk by the earthquakes, so what appears to be the base of a sandy canal was formed at a later time and is not the original..

It is difficult to say whether the stones were put there by men, or are natural, or are even the stones that fell down from the city itself, forming a ring of débris all around the base of the volcano — except that as far as débris goes, they are all perfectly rounded and graded to a large size on the outside of about 30 inches in diameter with a bed of about 30 inches of small stones underneath. One geological opinion considers this wall to be originally formed by lava flow which on cooling forms the rounded boulders.

The volcano itself could almost be considered to be two volcanoes. There is the steep sided central cone of lava which now exists on the south side of the volcano, and on the west, north and eastern flanks are three 'arms' forming a sort of 'cross' making a low plateau formed by lava flow.

On the northern 'arm' there exists a sandy embankment running across it but without the rounded stones found around the remainder of the volcano and on the eastern 'arm' there are various concentric ridges or 'rings of land', called by the experts 'gas flow ridges'.

The question of the soil is somewhat strange, since the entire volcano is covered in man-made terraces, and many of these terraces are now covered in sand. It seems illogical that someone would construct a terrace and then cover it with sand for cultivation, so the conclusion may be that the sand arrived after the terraces were built, and is evidence of the site being under the sea or perhaps what Plato called 'the shoal mud which the island threw up as it settled down' — in other words, fine particles brought to the surface by liquefaction.

A source of underground water rises within the central cone and one can almost imagine it being led to the ridges of land on the eastern wing creating a 'Grove of Poseidon'.

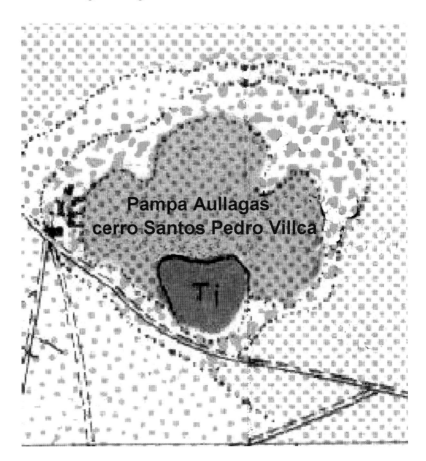

Fig. 8.01. The geology map shows the volcanic cone and lava-flow plateau forming the shape of a cross — origin of the 'Cross of the Andes' or even of the 'Maltese Cross'?

It is difficult to say whether there may have been more to the volcano on the southern side which was sunk by earthquakes. One has the feeling that on this side there may be a part missing, possibly even constructed embankments, but the rings of land and channels on the site are concentric one within the other and there is no better way to describe the formations in Pampa Aullagas. In any event the site also has the shape of the 'Cross of the Andes', and one could even go further than that since it also has the circular canals one might compare it more favourably to a Celtic cross, that is, a cross with a circle around its perimeter which is also what Ignatius Donnelly, in his *Atlantis: The Antediluvian World,* called the symbol of the Garden of Eden! (Donnelly 1949, p. 332)

Fig. 8.02. Detail of a 'Maltese Cross' found on a sculpture outside the Tiwanaku Institute.

Fig 8.03. The 'Celtic Cross' with the circular rings joining the arms of the cross.

Fig. 8.04. Christian crosses on the summit of the nearby volcano of Quillacas. Note the circle and the cross.

Fig. 8.05. The square-shaped Andean cross from Tiwanaku.

Fig. 8.06. 'Atlantis: where you find the secret of the history of the world' — poster by team LAMA highlighting the Andean Cross at Pampa Aullagas.

9. Stones and Cactus

Up to now I had made four visits to Bolivia. The first in 1995, a solo trip to look for the giant canal one stade wide to the west of Lake Poopó. Next in April 1998 with a BBC film crew and to rendez-vous with the Kota Mama expedition sailing their reed boats down the River Desaguadero from Lake Titicaca to Lake Poopó. Then in December of the same year with a film director from Atlantic Productions to recce some sites for a possible Atlantis film. This was the trip during which we visited the virtually unknown city of Pumiri, Volcán Quemado, the village of Chipaya and established the basis of 'The Atlantis Trail'.

In November of the year 2000, I was back with a film crew from Discovery Channel for the film "Atlantis in the Andes". This was the first, if somewhat brief, visit to Pampa Aullagas and about two years later the documentary was circulating around Bolivia as 'Atlántida en los Andes'.

As a result of the film 'Atlantis in the Andes', I was approached by Miguel Vargas Mújica of the Oruro Technical University to enter into a *Convenio* or agreement of co-operation to study all the aspects of the Altiplano and help promote tourism. While they were

Fig. 9.01. Red stone block on one of the rings of land at Pampa Aullagas.

Fig. 9.02. Luís Gutiérrez and Andro Suxs Vega camping on the Atlantis Trail.

busy organizing conferences and preparing my book *Atlantis: the Andes Solution* for publication in Bolivia, and also officially establishing the 'Atlantis Trail' intended as a newly created excursion for tourists, I received an email from tour guide Luís Gutiérrez Flores telling me he was proposing to cycle down to Pampa Aullagas with two of his colleagues and asking if I could give him any guidance or advice.

I asked him to keep an eye open for any cut stones, since on my return to England at the beginning of 2001 after the Discovery Channel expedition, studying many of the photos I had taken on site, it appeared there were numerous cut stones in various corners of the photos such as the red block in Figure 9.01.

On May 11, 2004, Luís with his two friends set off on the Atlantis Trail, cycling around the southern edge of the lake to arrive at Pampa Aullagas. The report they then sent me was full of enthusiasm recounting their great adventure and the many 'cut' stones they discovered all covered in 'coral' (actually accumulated lake deposits called *katawi)* from the time of the great lake inundation.

I advised them to take their findings to the local university and archaeology institutions but the archaeologists and anthropologists of these institutions rejected their findings and considered the stones not to be cut stones but natural products of the volcano.

Fig. 9.03. Looking into the inner sandy depression, descending from the central cone, what looked like cut stones could be seen in the lower corners of the photo.

Cut stones or natural lava?

On my Discovery Channel expedition I certainly recall seeing plenty of stones and cactus. But did we really expect to see cut stone platforms, the bases of ancient buildings or cut stone landing stages? I guess we did. But mostly we saw stone débris all over the place, many dry stone walls and plenty of cactus and sand.

But our brief visit with *Discovery* was only a reconnaissance and not an in-depth study. On the day of filming when we arrived, the village was busy having a fiesta out the back, and we did not have the benefit of someone from the village to guide us nor were we aware of the extent to which the volcano or *cerro* was actually 'inhabited'.

In fact there were drystone walls and fields all around us, and even now looking back at the photos taken on site, it is easy to see the outline of many drystone buildings or corrals which were not previously noticed.

Fig. 9.04. Cut stone from the mountain at Pampa Aullagas.

Fig. 9.05. One of the many varieties of beautiful coloured stones to be found on the site.

Fig. 9.06. One of the peculiarly curved stones.

Fig. 9.07. The author with one of the many peculiar stones found on the route ascending the volcano that here looks like part of a former statue.

Team LAMA, as Luís and his friends now styled themselves, continued with a further two expeditions crawling all over the volcano and discovering a variety of apparently cut stones of the most beautiful variety of colours.

Unfortunately the archaeologists and vulcanologists did not think the cut stones were cut at all, but rather examples of the typical 'blocky lava' which a volcano of this sort produces. Regarding the apparent sandstone, one vulcanologist said it was not sandstone at all but rather one of the many types of crystalline lava this volcano could produce, due to the varying percentage of gas in the lava at the time it was released from the volcano. He even went as far as to say that there was no sandstone in this region — something I found strange as the local museum in Oruro was full of carved sandstone llama heads from the Wankarani culture.

On the other hand he did agree that 'blocky lava' would be ideal material for building construction, and with the many varieties of beautiful colours available, they must indeed have been beautiful buildings.

In any case, Plato did not mention cut stones as such, merely that they mixed the variety of stones of red, black and white to give a pleasing appearance. Although beautifully cut stones are to be found at Tiwanaku, other buildings in the region vary from the rough stone constructions cemented together with the white lake deposit material such as may be found at Pumiri, to other types of wall consisting of natural uncut blocks, the natural flat surfaces of the stones being laid one on top of another.

Later opinions however, from a variety of persons including geologists and local miners were in favour that the stones were after all very obviously *cut* stones and one former rector of the local Oruro Technical University who previously worked in bridge construction actually knew the process whereby the stones were cut by using a chisel and tapping with a sharp blow on natural lines ingrained in the stones. I would point out additionally that we are not talking about cutting rectangular stone blocks as in the processes of today, but a technique where only the outward face of the stone is cut, the remainder of the stone being hidden in the construction, or sometimes a stone is cut with two or three faces if it occurs in a corner of a building.

But something which one vulcanologist did point out on examining the air photo was that the site had been inhabited for a very, very long time.

Other reports say that on the Altiplano, the mountain tops, that is, the volcanoes, were the first sites to be inhabited and considered 'sacred' ground, and this makes complete sense if we consider that in early times the water levels may have been substantially higher rendering the level pastures of today completely under water.

With periodic destructions by earthquakes, it is hard without detailed and thorough scientific investigation from multiple disciplines, that is, geologists as well as archaeologists, to determine what the original form of the volcano may have been and to what extend the walls, platforms and so on, may have been rebuilt over time.

Fig. 9.08. My young assistant points out a beautiful red stone on the mountain at Pampa Aullagas.

Fig. 9.09. One of the white stone blocks from the mountain at Pampa Aullagas.

Fig. 9.10. One of the black stones found high up on the mountainside at Cerro Santos Villca, Pampa Aullagas. Covered in fossilized lake deposits known as katawi it is also similar in style to the type of stone found at Tiwanaku.

10. An Invitation to Oruro

Following on from the *Convenio* with the Oruro Technical University (UTO), I was invited by them to travel to Oruro on November 1, 2004, to participate in a short series of conferences as part of the UNESCO 'catedra' and in association with the international *Expoteca* or exhibition centre which the University had organized.

I left Cambridge, England on October 30, not without some confusion since that was the very night the clocks changed at 0200 in the morning (going back one hour from British Summer Time to Greenwich Mean Time) and the coach to the airport was also scheduled to leave at 0200 in the morning. Fortunately a friend phoned me in advance to tip me off about the clock change, otherwise I would have been at the coach station one hour early and wondering what happened to the transportation!

I duly arrived in La Paz on October 31 after about a thirty-three hours journey to be met at the airport by John Villegas of Zingara Travel and Miguel Vargas of the Oruro Technical University.

John whisked me off to downtown La Paz where he had booked me into a superb suite at the Hotel Camino Real, courtesy of the Villegas family, for a spot of rest before beginning a day of TV and radio interviews. Then on the following day, November 1, it was down to Oruro for the series of conferences.

The conferences proved quite popular especially amongst the younger students and I am always open to questions or fresh input by any of the participants. One such question by one of the more mature audience was 'forget flooding on the Altiplano by the lakes Tauca, and so on — it is well known that the southern part of the Altiplano collapsed as it is supported on a gas bubble, could not that collapse have been the end of Atlantis?'

Well, it certainly could have been, and it makes absolute sense that that may well have been the main event which triggered the end of Atlantis. If we recall that the Altiplano has always been fairly level with originally a slight tilt so that the water may have drained to the north, then a sudden collapse of the region to the south would have reversed the water flow, perhaps even being the event referred to in 'The Legend of the Desaguadero' where the god Tunupa is said to have opened the mouth of the Desaguadero River in Lake Titicaca causing the water to flow south. Posnansky

Comparison of ancient and modern shorelines on the Altiplano

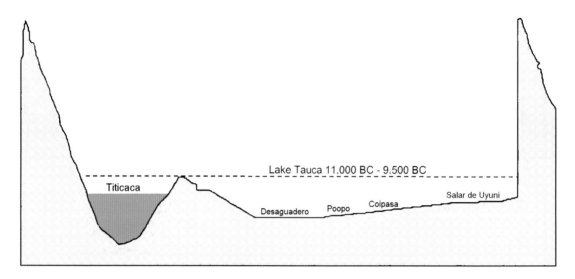

Fig. 10.01. Lake Tauca 16,000–13,000 bc followed by Lake Coipasa 11,000– 9,500 bc. The Desaguadero is horizontal and parallel to the lake level. Prior to the arrival of the lake, water drains from the Salar de Uyuni.

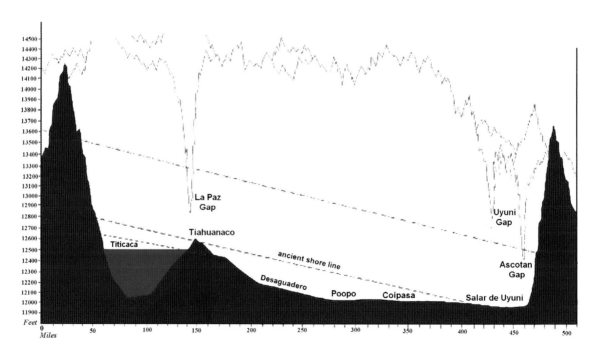

Fig. 10.02. Exaggerated section through the Altiplano showing ancient shore lines. Note the slant where land has sunk at the southern end and risen at the northern end. Source: Bellamy, Built before the Flood.

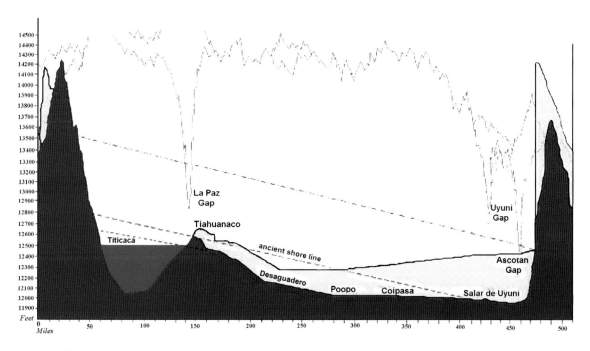

Fig. 10.03. Combining the two drawings shows how the land has sunk at the southern end.

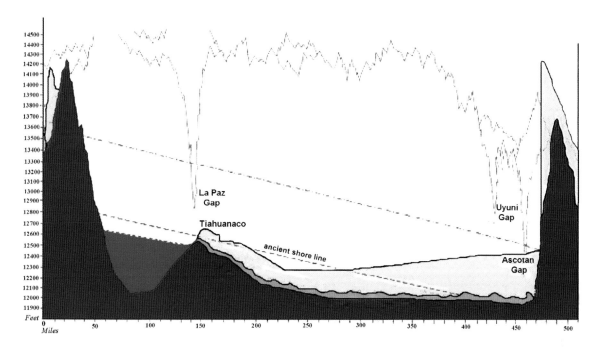

Fig. 10.04. If the land sank suddenly or even if just the alluvial plain around Pampa Aullagas dropped suddenly ... the water from Lake Titicaca would flow southwards in a giant tidal wave.

as part of his investigations at Tiwanaku followed the lake strand lines south for a distance of 400 km and was of the opinion that the northern part of the Altiplano rose due to the melting of glacial ice, which also filled Lake Titicaca. He thought that this could either have been 'in a violent manner or through successive modifications' with most of the rising of the land being a gradual process and followed by another 'enigmatic inclination a short time ago' (Posnansky 1947).

The land around Pampa Aullagas is composed of alluvial deposits from the lake and materials washed down from the mountains, so that, irrespective of a gradual process in the elevation of the general landmass to the north, earthquakes could have caused this material to consolidate and sink in elevation in a sudden event. A sudden collapse of the southern region and sudden flow of water may have resulted in a giant tidal wave or *tsunami* which could have wiped out everything in the southern area exactly as Plato said 'in a single day and night of earthquakes and floods' and when the water finally dissipated there would be no corroborating evidence such as in the tidal marks left around the shores of the Altiplano by the ancient lakes.

This may also help explain why the surrounding perimeter wall at a distance of 50 stades from the central island has completely disappeared — except for a small portion which exists on the side towards Quillacas, in other words on the side which would have been sheltered from the main force of any tidal wave.

The huge destructive power of these natural events is all too clear to us today as, at the very time I am writing these notes, December 27, 2004, *tsunamis* caused by underwater earthquakes off the northern coast of Indonesia, have just hit the coastal regions of India and Thailand, resulting in massive destruction and the deaths of many thousands of people.

It is logical that apart from the reverse of water from the Titicaca scenario outlined

Fig. 10.05. This drawing by René Rojas from Legends of Bolivia by Antonio Paredes-Candia shows the God of the Andes punishing the city of Tiahaunacu for falling into evil ways — not just a parallel to the Atlantis story but surely the origin of the Atlantis story.

above, any earthquakes in the region of Pampa Aullagas could equally result in *tsunamis* on the Altiplano given that, formerly, it had a much higher level of water systems and lakes.

Finding cut stones

After the various conferences arranged by UTO, we had planned a three-day expedition to Pampa Aullagas and the region, but first we had a brief one-day excursion to the site with two coachloads of students and visitors from the UNESCO catedra.

The priorities seemed to be more to escort and guide the visitors rather than to carry out more original explorations, but on climbing the mountain, it was the 'tourists' themselves who seemed eagerly to find all the remnants of cut stones.

Then right on top of the central cone, I noticed a crowd gathered round one of our guests, Ernesto Thofehrn who was crouched over a hole in the ground with headphones glued to his head. He gesticulated me over. 'Here try these' he said, handing me the headphones. The other end of the lead had a microphone lowered inside the hole. 'You can hear the sound of water below'. And indeed it was so. Evidence at last that Plato's story of the sources of water on top of the mountain was true.

After descending the scenic route from the volcano we headed out into the Altiplano a short distance where we found more pools of water bubbling up from the ground to the great delight of all our visitors. The locals claim to live to one hundred years old by drinking this water, said to be the elixir of life or a fountain of eternal youth on account of the mineral properties. One of them explained enthusiastically, 'You know there is a whirlpool in Lago Aullagas (Lake Poopó). The water enters there and comes out in the Pacific'. Maybe that's what 'The Legend of the Desaguadero' meant when it said the god Tunupa (or Poseidon) drowned and disappeared under the waters of the Aullagas.

After the 'guided tour' on the Friday, we were scheduled to return the following Monday for a three-day exploration with one of the UTO jeeps. Alas, by four in the afternoon the jeep still had not turned up. Fortunately Alfredo Villca, the *consejo* or regional official, was with us in the hotel and quickly arranged with the *Prefectura* (the equivalent of the County Hall) for the loan of a jeep for three days.

Fig. 10.06. Typical of the cut stones partly buried in the ground.

Fig. 10.07. Cut stone from the mountain at Pampa Aullagas.

Fig. 10.08. Typical of the cut stones to be found re-used amongst the later drystone walls.

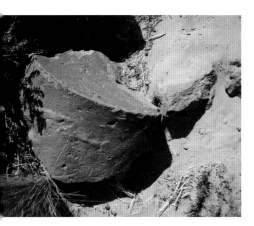

Fig. 10.09. One of the stones that looks like part of a column.

So it was not until around 8.15 pm that evening that we arrived again at Pampa Aullagas. This, however, meant we could make an early start the next morning, the team comprising myself, Luís Gutiérrez — tourist guide and *aficionado* of Pampa Aullagas — his two friends who had formed the team LAMA (one an archaeologist and the other, Andro Suxs Vega, who had heard of the expedition and made his own way to nearby Quillacas and walked from there to Pampa Aullagas) and finally, Alfredo Villca.

The object was to look for any cut stones that could be found on site and generally do a recce for any signs of Atlantis, and generally to get a feel for the place. We also wished to explore the circular channels, both their exact location and any onsite evidence as to whether they even existed at all. It has to be remembered that, although not huge, the area is still large enough to take some time

Fig. 10.10. Luís Gutiérrez holds up one of the cut stones found scattered around the site.

to get familiar with. Also we wanted to scout out any interesting features that might be included on future tourist trails around the volcano.

We set out around 7 am, first climbing the steep rocky wall of the outer embankment behind the village. On the top of this embankment on the air photo could be seen the outline of a sort of inner platform and this is what we found on top, a kind of level platform with what looked like the base of an inner fortification consisting now of rough black stones. We descended the gully on

Fig. 10.11. One of the cut stones found scattered around the site.

Fig. 10.13. Cold springs on the plain near Pampa Aullagas.

Fig. 10.12. Ernesto Thofehrn (left) points out the water source on the summit of the volcano.

Fig. 10.14. Katawi or fossilized lake deposits cover the outer ring wall or embankment at Pampa Aullagas.

the inner side and followed it along to the gap between the two outer embankments, then followed another 'track' which it seemed appropriate to baptize the 'Route of Orichalcum' before arriving at a broad sandy bay easily comparable to any in Ibiza or Mallorca and which also spurred to mind a romantic title such as 'Bahía de las Ninfas' or 'Playa de las Ninfas' (Bay of the Nymphs, or Beach of the Nymphs).

We had seen a few suitable 'nymphs' at the UTO Expoteca exposition clad in gold and silver costumes and we thought it appropriate that Atlantis should also have its *Diosa del Oro* (Golden Goddess) and *Diosa de Plata* (Silver Goddess) and a whole host of other Copper or Orichalcum Goddesses or Goddesses of the Moon and of the Stars and of the Galaxy, and so on.

But right now it was a pretty empty sandy beach and we would have to bring along our own goddesses another time in the future.

Crossing the Bahía de las Ninfas we approached one of our major objectives, namely, to see if the ring of land continued on the northern side of the volcano as it appeared to do on the air photo. Indeed it did, except that this time it did not have the outer wall of stone on the side facing the lake. Perhaps the stones had disappeared due to the earthquakes but certainly it was a formidable embankment of sand, with an elevation of 12,480 ft making it about 480 ft above the surrounding level plain. We continued along the embankment until we reached another little bay which it seemed appropriate this time to name *Puerto de la Atlántida* (Atlantis Harbour).

Beyond this we found another little route leading up onto the continuation of the volcano and we could easily imagine this as being the *Ruta de los Esclavos* (Slaves' Route) with on the left a conglomeration of giant rounded *katawi*-like fossilized corals which looked suitable for a *Torre de las Vírgenes* (Virgins' Tower)

Fig. 10.15. The 'Playa de las Ninfas' (Nymphs' Beach).

with on the right a giant stone ball split in the centre like some giant egg left behind by an equally mysterious giant bird — only the name *Huevo del Roc* (Roc's Egg) would serve!

From the touristic point of view, it certainly sounded much more appealing to talk of looking for the 'Roc's Egg' or visiting the Bahía de las Ninfas than merely saying, Visit the stone in square E14 or the sandy bay in L14.

We made the circuit of the entire volcano, returning to the south side where we began an ascent of this more difficult face.

On the way, we encountered at a level of around 400 ft the upper limit of the *katawi*, the stones covered in white lake deposits showing the upper limits of the lake levels. Beyond that on our way to the summit we encountered innumerable drystone walls and level platforms or terraces — the higher altitude making it more like 'the Eagle's Nest' — but showing that there must have been considerable inhabitation of this volcano at some date, or that is to say, reoccupation by later cultures.

And on the top itself we came to a level platform in the shape of the cross — the Andean cross with arms of equal length although part of it had been ravaged by time and fallen away down the hill. Taking this to be the very summit of Atlantis, let me give you the coordinates as recorded by the GPS:

067° 02.955' West, 18° 11.975' South, elevation 12,911 ft.

Luís heroically carried my heavy camera bag without complaint over all these rocks and crags for the entire expedition — a full nine-hour day — and when on the highest point of the volcano asked me, 'Would you like a drink, Mister? I'll run back down to the village and get one for you!'

I declined his kind offer, amazed that after making a full circuit of the volcano and climbing the steep southern face, he had the energy to even think of 'running back down to the village and then running back up again!'

We crossed over to the alternative but lower summit on which sits the chapel to St Michael then descended by the usual tourist route which is the normal path leading to the village. At the foot of the central cone we came to the inner ring of sand and followed it along a short way around the base of the cone. In this region amongst the many drystone walls, we found many fragments of stones that looked cut and polished, possibly fragments from former buildings

One particular fragment which caught my attention had the curved and sculpted form as if part of a pillar or rather the under-

Fig. 10.16. Diosa del oro (goddess of gold) — one of the 'nymphs' of Atlantis!

Fig. 10.17. Alfredo Villca with one of the terrace walls.

Fig. 10.18. One of the many terraces with oustanding view of the Plain and the Sea.

side of the capital of a pillar, and I do not think there could be any question but this fragment had been made by the hand of man as opposed to nature.

We also visited again the segment of what looked like the perimeter wall halfway between Pampa Aullagas and Quillacas and re-examined the lines of *katawi* found on the top. If inside each *katawi* there was an elongated stone then these must be remnants of stone walls that lined the top of this embankment and since the embankment was otherwise made of sand, these must be the remains of the structures which Plato said were to be found there.

The next day on our way returning to Oruro we made a brief stop at Quillacas to inquire of someone who had reportedly found some stone tablets nearby. Unfortunately the required person was away working in the fields at the time, but the *alcalde* (mayor) and governors turned out and told us that under the village there had been another city whose stones had been used to build the original village of Quillacas. They even took us to a house that was being built and showed us one of the original large square stones from an old city that had existed in the past, and explained that under all the present houses were walls of fine stones. Then they showed us a lined stone well and explained how it was connected by a system of underground tunnels to all the other wells in the village.

Fig. 10.19. Retaining wall near the summit.

Fig. 10.20. The entire site is covered in levelled platforms for cultivation.

I felt the whole trip had been extremely worthwhile. The predominant feature of Plato's island of Atlantis was the concentric rings of land and we had found a further ring of land on the northern side of the island, another continuation of the canal-like channel which could correspond to a ring of water. In addition, we had discovered sources of water on top of the volcano, cut stones all around the volcano, more water springs on the plain, and another ancient city under Quillacas which again should not be surprising since Quillacas was also at one time the capital of a localised federation of small states. A further interesting find was still to come. On our return to Oruro, I was shown the remains of mastodons that workmen had found while digging a new road to the west of the city.

Fig. 10.21. All of the terraces or platforms are now covered in sand — brought in by the sea or due to the process of earthquakes? Could this be what Plato called 'the shoal mud which the island threw up as it settled down'?

A few days later and the Expoteca had finished. The Oruro Technical University could now fulfil its promise of lending me a jeep and kindly provided a vehicle, driver and gasoline for three days to go anywhere I wanted.

Fig. 10.22. Remains of embankment similar to the perimeter wall which Plato said enclosed the city complex at a distance of '50 stades' from the central island.

Fig. 10.23. One of the stones of an ancient city uncovered whilst constructing a modern house in Quillacas.

Fig. 10.24. On top of the sandy embankment is a line of stone covered in katawi.

I had a route in mind. First of all, a few months earlier Luís had sent me some information on a 'fish-like' mummy which existed in a town called Pisiga on the Bolivian side of the border with Chile on the far west side of the Altiplano. If this mummy existed, it was too important a discovery not to be investigated.

Fig. 10.25. Remains of one of the stone walls covered in katawi found on top of the perimeter embankment.

Fig. 10. 26. Stone block from former constructions found at Pampa Aullagas.

11. Completing the Trail

My aim was to go first to investigate the mummy found at Pisiga. I then intended to follow the Atlantis Trail and cross the Salar de Coipasa southwards to a village called Tres Cruces where some cyclists a few years earlier had sent me a report of a continuation of the giant canal. Then I would return towards Pampa Aullagas and investigate what looked like a similar volcano called Cerro Salli Kkolla in the region west of Pampa Aullagas. This volcano on the satellite image also appeared to have a ring of land and the only way to find out and to eliminate all possibility of other volcanoes with rings of land in the region was to visit it on site and see for myself.

Then the return to Oruro was to be by the west side of the lake, passing by Andamarca and the giant canal section I had visited on my first trip way back in 1995.

We stocked up with provisions on the way out of Oruro and set off along the newly metalled highway which existed only as far as Toledo, then the jeep took to the desert, it being easier to ride along the sandy surface of the plain than suffer the boneshaking experience of the base of the future road which was being built westwards towards Chile.

Some three hours later we rolled into the village of Huachacalla where my good friend Max Biggemann had told me there was to be found an interesting little museum belonging to the religious order living there, and which housed some curious pottery. We found the church. We found the museum. But we could not find the museum keeper. We were told that that personage had taken himself off for the day to some other village in the distance and therefore no one had the key.

So it was on to Pisiga. We passed the immense and picturesque volcano of Tata Sabaya, its top crowned with volcanic débris from 'recent' eruptions and descended past the fringes of the salt lake and into Pisiga.

The mummy was kept in the Alcaldía so we drew up in front of that building. But there was no *alcalde* so Luís went off to fetch the *alcalde*'s daughter who we presumed would have the key. I waited in the square dressed in my honorary poncho outfit presented by the people of Pampa Aullagas and felt rather like Clint Eastwood awaiting the arrival of Lee Van Cleef ready for a gunfight around

Fig. 11.01. View looking over one
of the great Salars (salt flats).

the plaza. Music blared out from a *cantina* on the side of the square where some people must have been having a good time.

A rather attractive *señorita* sauntered across the square, her broad sombrero pulled down to shade her flashing eyes. I sort of wished I really were Clint Eastwood in some Western film and we were doing things differently ...

Instead, after what seemed ages, Luis returned with the *alcalde's* daughter who led us into the building. Alas, she explained, the *alcalde* was the only one who had the key and he was away visiting another town.

She handed us instead a shiny tourist brochure which recommended we visit another museum in the village so I asked if instead we could visit that one. 'Sorry, *señor,*' she replied, 'the owner of that museum is also away in another town and no one else has the key'.

I concluded that that must be the standard reply for tourists in the Altiplano. In an area which desperately needs tourists, you can't visit the attractions because, quote, 'the owner is away and is the only person with the key'.

Well, if I can't recommend Pisiga on account of its mummy, then at least I can recommend it on account of its attractive señoritas or, should I say, *señoritas bonitas.*

It seems there had originally been three of the fish-head mummies in Pisiga, but the people got frightened by their spirits residing in the village so returned two of them to their ancestral burial-tombs, or *chulpas.* A young boy offered to guide us to the site of the *chulpas* which was on the edge of the salar. It took around half an hour to get there and we found the region to be covered by a series of small islands which might have originally been suitable for habitation, but the *chulpas* were set back from the edge of the salar on the mainland.

Briefly looking inside one of the chulpa entrances we found only a pile of disturbed bones and rotting flesh, nothing worth tarrying for, so we hastily took the boy back to the village of Pisiga before pressing on to cross the salar in the direction of the village of Coipasa.

As it was, a single mummy of fish-like features did not have the same archaeological appeal as three such specimens since one could always claim it was freak of nature or of faulty mummification. But apart from the fish-like aspect of the head, we were told that the mummies also had *webbed hands,* that is, with membranes between the fingers. That is to say we were talking about a possibly unknown other species of human which had existed on the

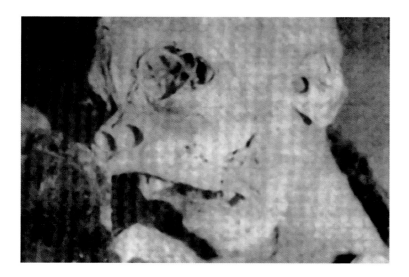

Fig. 11.02. Photo of mummy in Pisiga. Source: La Prensa.

Altiplano in the remote past and who could be perhaps the ancestors of the Urus, since the Urus were known to live amongst the shallow waters as presumably did these fish-like specimens. In fact the name *Uru* was given them by the Aymaras and means 'the most ancient peoples', though other accounts say *uru* is a corruption of the Spanish *oro* meaning gold since it was thought by the conquistadors that these Urus had stocks of gold. In their own language their name is *Kot'suñs* which means *water men*. And that should not really be so strange considering the Altiplano was covered by a series of shallow lakes over a period of many thousands of years.

And this brings me to my other favourite connection — the Sumerians who are said to have arrived at the entrance to the river Euphrates with a ready made civilization and no one knows where they came from. In Mesopotamia, the early Sumerians are said to have arrived by sea and were an aquatic people, in the beginning the early settlers lived amongst the marshes and used reed boats not unlike those of Lake Titicaca and Lake UruUru (a continuation of Lake Poopó).

The Sumerians built a city called Ur and their name for the river Euphrates was Urutu meaning 'copper river', yet there was no copper or any other metals in the region, so the river was used to import metals from overseas. It is not hard to guess where the metals came from.

It is known they had a fish-like god called *Oannes,* known as bringer of civilization, who is described in detail by the third century BC Babylonian writer Berossus:

At Babylon there was (in these times) a great resort of people of various nations, who inhabited Chaldea, and lived in a lawless manner like the beasts of the field. In the first year there appeared, from that part of the Erythraen sea which borders upon Babylonia, an animal endowed with reason, by name Oannes, whose whole body (according to the account of Apollodorus) was that of a fish, that under the fish's head he had another head, with feet also below, similar to those of a man, subjoined to the fish's tail. His voice too, and language, was articulated and human, and a representation of him is preserved even to this day.

This Being was accustomed to pass the day amongst men: but took no food at that season: and he gave them an insight into letters and sciences, and arts of every kind. He taught them to construct cities, to found temples, to compile laws, and explained to them the principles of geometrical knowledge. He made them distinguish the seeds of the earth, and shewed them how to collect the fruits; in short, he instructed them in everything which could tend to soften manners and humanize their lives. From that time, nothing material has been added by way of improvement to his instructions. And when the sun had set, this Being Oannes, retired again into the sea, and passed the night in the deep; for he was amphibious. After this there appeared other animals like Oannes.

(Berossus, from *Ancient Fragments,* ed. Isaac Preston Cory)

Fig. 11.03. The Sumerian fish-god, Oannes, drawing by Faucher-Gudin from an Assyrian bas-relief at Nimrud. Source: G.Maspero.

Another of their deities was *Enki* (not too different from *Inki* or *Inca*), like Poseidon, the god of the sea, who is said to have taught them how to build canals to irrigate the level plain they lived upon. He arrived on a reed ship with high prow and stern.

Poseidon, incidentally, apart from being commonly known as the god of the sea was also a metallurgist, creator of earthquakes and a *benefactor to mankind.*

When Noah built his Ark to escape the flood (originally a Sumerian or Chaldean legend, part of the cycle of stories concerning Gilgamesh, king of Uruk) he built a giant reed ship. The dimensions given in the Bible, can be demonstrated to be those of a standard Sumerian reed ship.

Fig. 11.04. *Chulpa* or burial tomb, typical of this region of the Altiplano.

What is interesting here is that the 'Sumerians' who settled in Mesopotamia, now southern Iraq, had a culture very similar to that of the Uru, the people who lived on the Bolivian Altiplano all along the aquatic axis of the river Desaguadero from Lake Titicaca to Lake Poopó and who were said to be the people of the dawn or the first people. The Uru lived on floating islands made of bundles of reeds tied together. Today what is left of these people still live on floating islands in Lake Titicaca and in the remote village of Chipaya in the middle of the level Altiplano, now more or less a desert, west of Lake Poopó. Their little round huts stand only a few inches above the level of the plain which is often flooded, so they live in the midst of the waters and are an 'aquatic' people.

Crossing the Salar de Coipasa

We had hoped to spend the night in Coipasa village in a former geologists' camp but it turned out not to have been occupied for years, so in the end with darkness falling sharply a villager known to the driver offered us one of the rooms in his house as an alternative to a night on the cold and windswept Altiplano.

Next morning it was time for another early start, crossing the salt desert known as the Salar de Coipasa in the direction of Tres Cruces, truly an Otherworld experience and a journey of a lifetime. We could see remote islands with cactus the only inhabitants in regions where few had boldly gone before at least not for thousands of years.

Arriving on the side of Tres Cruces we were suddenly surrounded by vehicles speeding off in all directions. '*Contrabandistas,*' murmured our driver.

We spent some time scouting around for the section of canal that the cyclists had mentioned and in the location they gave, left the jeep on the side of the salar for a scouting session inland. After maybe an hour or so we came across a large flat bed gully which looked like it could be the aforementioned canal or channel. We followed it a way 'upstream' only to find it nothing more than the bed of a stream but following it downwards again in the direction of the jeep I came to a branch or turn off which looked like the section of canal the cyclist spoke of. Only again there was little time to follow it across the mountains to see if it emerged on the side of the Salar de Uyuni. That would have to be for a future expedition.

What struck me most about Tres Cruces, the tiny little hamlet on the southern side of the Salar de Coipasa, was the sheer natural beauty of the place and the warm sheltered welcoming feeling that it had. I was struck, too, with the fact that, as with all these remote mountains in the wild Altiplano, the nearby mountain tops had at some time in the past been cultivated right up to their highest point, for there remained the evidence of ancient boundary walls covering all of them in places today so inaccessible that no-one would think of bothering to go there or to suffer the hardship of climbing them.

Returning in the direction of Pampa Aullagas there was not much of a road to follow, only a dirt track which meant hours of jolting around in the jeep.

At one location about halfway along, we saw what looked in the distance like a flat-topped pyramid and when we approached it turned out to be more of a grass-covered mountain — but who knows what could lay beneath considering the pyramid of Akapana in Tiwanaku has been covered by earth and dirt for centuries.

We arrived at our destination of Cerro Salli Kkolla to find a more or less conical volcano with a flattened platform on top, several stone walls and a covering of *katawi,* but nothing as impressive as Pampa Aullagas and only one type of volcanic stone, proving that Pampa Aullagas was something unique in the area. I had felt it important to check out any comparative volcanoes in the region in a final process of elimination.

It was just before dusk when we arrived back at Pampa Aullagas to find that John Villegas had sent a first batch of tourists down there, and three jeeps were encamped on the side of the river Laca Jahuira.

We were given a warm welcome and invited to join the camp fire and participate in a glass of beer which was much needed after a whole day in the dusty jeep.

The following day, we managed to visit another volcano and attractive village site at Cerro Gloria Pata where there was also what looked like an artificial mound by the side of the main volcano and a section of cave-like dwellings for former troglodytes. Then we had a journey of a few more hours before we made it back to Oruro.

The main accomplishment of this trip had been to identify a few villages where in the future it might be suitable to build a few badly needed guest lodges around the Atlantis Trail to open up this most beautiful and wild section of Bolivia to tourism, since there was no need for the many tourists to head all the way south to the Salar de Uyuni when an even more scenic route lay right on the doorstep of Oruro.

12. From Tarija to Tiwanaku

A few extra days were spent further to the south in Tarija first of all to visit the mastodon skeletons which were in the large museum there (fortunately it was open to the public and there was no need to look for the key!) and chance also brought us to a private museum belonging to Oscar Varas Castrillo who had created the Fundación Varascas to show off his private collection of artefacts. Among the exhibits was an amazing three-dimensional wall showing life in the region as it had been thousands of years ago according to the fossil record, with projecting mammoth tusks and depictions of sabre-toothed tigers. It looked like a total delight for children and adults alike who could also take advantage of the Tarija sun to take a dip in the museum's private swimming pool — surely the only museum in the world which boasts a swimming pool and a tropical garden as well as a Hawaiian style beach hut.

Fig. 12.01. Mastodon remains in the museum in Tarija.

Next day we were invited to join Oscar and his companions for a tour of an Inca city at El Saire, a site covering some forty hectares in the most beautiful countryside about one and a half hours by jeep from Tarija.

We entered a dried-up river valley that would have done proud to a typical Mediterranean landscape, then climbed an eroded canyon wall to find ourselves on a small platform with the walled outline of a tiny settlement. I wondered if that was all there was and if it was worth coming for, but then we proceeded onwards and upwards until a vast site revealed itself. Set in an incredibly beautiful landscape was acre upon acre of what must have been a city of considerable population, but now all that remained was thousands of rectangular and flattish stones strewn all over the mountain top. It was amazing how there was not a single wall left standing although, here and there, one could discern what would have been foundations of walls at some remote time or another.

Fig. 12.02. Remains of the Inca city at Saire.

Presumably the city had just fallen down due to the passage of time or perhaps aided by earth tremors or earthquakes. But the damage was not on a large scale of devastation or convulsion. It was easy to picture how the stones of Atlantis must have similarly fallen down only then to be swallowed up by the earth which, in the case of the Pampa Aullagas site, had an underlying water table unlike this mountain top site.

The sharp eyes of Don Oscar picked out a half-buried stone arrow point, about half an inch long, which he proudly presented me with.

Later, back in the museum, he showed me something rather more precious and interesting of which he was justifiably proud and which I found spellbinding and fascinating. These were three stone statues 14 inches in height, two of which reminded me more of the Olmec culture — said to be one of the earliest civilizations in Mexico, and famous for small, polished stone statuettes — than anything I had seen in Bolivia. But, along with the third, they were still in the style of Tiwanaku (formerly spelled *Tiahuanacu*).

Don Oscar was of the opinion that these fine works of art had been not sculpted but made in some secret moulding process which he was reluctant to explain to us. He and his friend archaeologist Nelson were keen to stress, however, the number of ancient Inca and other cities and artefacts to be found in the region, which they claimed had received little attention from the archaeologists in La Paz, including one city which was said to be the 'Machu Picchu' of Bolivia.

In fact, Bolivia is a fabulous place for lovers of lost or little known pre-Columbian cities. Another little visited pre-Columbian city or citadel said to resemble Machu Picchu exists on the Atlantis Trail a few kilometres north of Salinas de Garci Mendoza. Set amongst breathtaking mountain landscape, the entrance to the citadel of Alcaya (19° 37.312´South 067° 43.641´West) is in a lush green valley where the visitor is first impressed by the ancient walled terraces, then makes an upward climb amongst the remains of rectangular or square bases of former stone-built houses with views of the valleys below and the overhanging mountains above.

In little niches here and there in the mountain crags are to be found the artefacts of these ancient peoples: ceramics, textiles, weapons and most famously, the mummies of the peoples themselves, promoted by the tourist office in Oruro as 'the famous mummies of Alcaya' gazing out for eternity from their mountain perches.

Descending from the mountain heights and returning to the bottom of the mountain fortress one comes to an overgrown garden amongst retaining walls at the base of a cliff face where crystal clear water trickles into a stone-built bath, ideal for cooling off from the heat of the day in a lost paradise.

The visit to Alcaya was courtesy of the CAINCO, a chamber of Commerce in Santa Cruz which was keen to assist with the development of the area, and transportation was in one of their three jeeps.

Not too far north of Alcaya, on the eastern side of the Salar de Coipasa lie three curious volcanoes in a row only a few miles apart.

Fig. 12.03. One of the sculptures found near Tarija.

Fig. 12.04. Valley and ruined walls at Alcaya.

Fig. 12.05. The mummies of Alcaya.

Fig. 12.06. This large model of Abora II shows four guara boards forward and two aft. When lowered into the water they help to prevent the ship drifting sideways. Raising the forward boards will turn the boat away from the wind or alternatively, raising the aft boards will turn the boat into the wind.

I had already visited the most southerly of these, Cerro Salli Kkolla, and planned to visit the other two but due to the distances involved was not able to make the journey at that time.

Later, reports began to come in of another citadel with cut stone blocks on the most northerly of the three volcanoes, Cerro San Martin, at 19º 16.5´ South, 067º 35´ West. By this time I had already left the Oruro area and was in La Paz preparing to return to England after a seven month stay in Bolivia.

Unexpectedly I had a phone call from Ricardo Ortiz of the Santa Cruz CAINCO telling me that a German scientist, Dominique Görlitz, was coming over to Bolivia to supervize the building of a

38 ft reed boat at Huatajata, and asking if I could take him for a visit to Pampa Aullagas. I decided to postpone my flight and met up with Dominique and his cameraman for a quick tour of the site.

Dominique was originally a botanist who had noticed that around 6000–3000 bc, several plants native to Africa were to be found in the Americas and similarly, several plants native to the Americas had been found in Africa.

He was particularly interested in reed boat navigation, and following in the footsteps of Thor Heyerdhal, had built two reed-boats, Abora I and II which had successfully navigated around the Mediterranean.

Dominique's reed boat designs were based upon rock drawings of reed boats found in the upper Nubian desert, said to date from 3600 to 3000 bc, that is, predating Egyptian culture.

The success and manoeuvrability of his boats were due to the incorporation of *guaras* or daggerboards which help prevent the boat drifting sideways also when raised or lowered, alter the centre of gravity of the vessel relative to the sail, allowing the boat to be turned into or away from the wind.

With the use of these *guara* boards, Abora II was able to sail seventy degrees into the wind. The *guaras* could be clearly seen on the ancient rock drawings, and Dominique told me also of similar drawings found in caves in Spain said to date to 12,000–15,000 bc, suggesting deep-sea navigation by an unknown pre-ice age culture.

We had only one day in Pampa Aullagas before returning to Oruro and La Paz, where Dominique was building Abora III with the intention of sailing from New York to the Canary Islands to prove the feasibility of a North Atlantic crossing route.

After the visit of Dominique to Pampa Aullagas, my assistant Luís Gutiérrez stayed on in the village so next day he could get the bus to Salinas, and from there made a five-hour walk to San Martín. He found the volcanic mountain to be surrounded by circular stone terraces and also covered in *katawi,* but lacking the circular canals formation which made Pampa Aullagas the unique location of Atlantis.

So San Martín, eliminated as the actual Atlantis site, remained another potentially interesting site for future visits on the Atlantis Trail.

The Tiwanaku calendar

Back in La Paz, Freddy Arce of the Tiwanaku Institute took me together with a group of Andean researchers for a visit to the ruins at Tiwanaku which had received government funding and were in the process of excavation. There was still much to uncover, but on one side of the Akapana pyramid a stone stairway and terrace had been laid bare while on the opposite side of the monument two separate layers of pyramid were visible. The opinion was that it could have been reconstructed in two separate stages, one phase being later than the other and one part possibly having been under water.

Freddy told me the overall dimensions of the pyramid, which is in fact a sort of 'T' shape. One side, he said was 210 metres (688.9 ft) I pulled out my pocket calculator as that number sounded familiar. A quick analysis showed that 210 metres was 400 Egyptian royal cubits of 525 mm (20.67 inches) or one Egyptian royal stadium.

The other side was 194.4 metres (637.8 ft). A quick calculation again revealed that 194.4 metres was 432 Egyptian geographic cubits of 450 mm (17.7 inches).

The Akapana is not alone in being constructed using 'Egyptian' royal cubits. The writings of Arthur Posnansky tell of a building similar to the Kalasasaya (the semi-sunken temple in Tiwanaku) which he records as existing on the island of Similake in the entrance to the Desaguadero River (Posnansky 1937). According to Posnansky, this structure has sides measuring 30 *loka* of 175 cm (68.9 inches). This would make the overall length 52.5 metres (172.24 ft) which is 100 Egyptian royal cubits of 525 mm (20.67 inches).

The relation between the geographic cubit and the royal cubit was that the geographic cubit consisted of 6 palms of 75 mm (3 inches) and the royal cubit had an extra palm of 75 mm making 7 palms to the cubit. This was the metric equivalent (derived from the Earth's circumference) of the 'pure' cubit of 21 inches (derived from the Earth's diameter) comprising 7 palms of 3 inches and the 'pure' geographic cubit comprising 6 palms of 3 inches. Note that the 3 inch cube when filled with water was the original pint of 16 fluid ounces, had a total of 64 cubic 'digits' and was the origin of the 1 lb weight so that a cubic foot of water was intended to be 64 pints or 64 lbs instead of the illogical 62.4 lbs we have at present. The ancient Egyptians used a cubic geographic foot divided into 64 pints, while some other ancient civilizations such as the Sumerians preferred to count by sixties and divided the cubic foot into 60 pints and thence into 60 shekels.

The relevance here is that it is not known who surveyed the Earth and originated the inch and measures based upon the inch such as the 'English' foot, the great cubit and sacred cubit. Could it have been the ancient Egyptians or the Sumerians? Certainly no one in Medieval England was aware that the inch was derived from the polar diameter of the planet and the 30 inch great cubit and 25 inch sacred cubit which are based upon this system were preserved in Ezekiel's description in the Bible. What makes it particularly interesting in our context, is that Hyatt and Ruth Verrill, writing in *America's Ancient Civilizations,* say that the smallest Inca measuring unit was a *yuka* of 5 inches and there were also multiples such as the *sikia* of 30 inches and *rikra* of 75 inches. Should this be confirmed it would be indeed most remarkable, meaning that the inch may have originated in South America, that is, Atlantis, since the *sikia* was none other than the great cubit and the *rikra* the same as three sacred cubits. That is why it is important one day to determine what units of measurement were actually used in South America, whether in fact inches, Sumerian units, or Egyptian cubits, or native American units or combinations of any of these.

The 21 inch cubit also served as the diameter of a wheel used for measuring distances, rolling out a Sumerian double yard of 66 inches, which is 100 Sumerian *shusi.* 120 revolutions would measure the Sumerian furlong of 660 English feet or 600 Sumerian feet.

If the Andean measurement unit was a *loka* of 175 cm as suggested by Posnansky then its correct interpretation and significance may have escaped previous investigators. Put simply, three *loka* of 175 cm are equal to 10 Egyptian royal cubits of 525 mm. Arthur Posnansky began studying Tiwanaku in 1904 and in 1945 published his monumental work *Tihuanacu, the Cradle of American Man.* He thought Tiwanaku had been constructed in three distinct stages or periods and gives the value of a *loka* according to each period (Vol. II, Chapter II, E, note 73). But his figures seem to be inconsistent since he begins:

> The *loka* of the First Period of Tihuanacu was 174 cm
> as can be seen clearly in the preglacial building on
> the island of Similake in the Desaguadero River (cf.
> Posnansky *Antropología y Sociología Andina,* 1937).

Then he states:

> ... each *loka* of the First Period measures 175 cm.
> The building of Similake has thirty *loka* of the First
> Period. In the Second Period ... it seems that the
> *loka* had the same size of 175 cm as in the First
> Period. With regard to the *loka* of the Third Period of
> Tihuanaku, it is only 161.51 cm.

Posnansky thought that the change of length in the *loka,* which he considered to have an 'anthropological origin', was due to the length of an arm span of one of the local inhabitants from fingertip to fingertip, and the reduced size resulted from the reduced stature of the inhabitants of the Third Period.

An alternative explanation might be that the original units were lost over time and different units used by different builders in different phases of construction, not all of whom may have had an interest in using an accurate system of measurement. But when some distances turn out to be in round numbers such as 100, 360, 400 or 432 of units found in the Old World, it does suggest that a scientific method of planning was used instead of the oft-quoted arm's length casually promoted by some researchers.

In the final editing of this book, I have only just come across Posnansky's figures for Tiwanaku itself, and, as there seem to be some inconsistencies in Posnansky's figures and his attempts to establish the *loka*, we can look at them again.

His reduced size for the value of the *loka* seems to be based on a measurement of a row of eleven pillars in the Kalasasaya temple which is assumed to be an ancient calendar of Tiwanaku. Posnansky measured from the centre of the first pillar 'A' to the centre of the last pillar 'K' and found the distance to be: '48 m 45 cm 7.5 mm which, divided by thirty normal measurements would give the figure of 161.51 which would be the true average of the metre of Tihuanacu of the Third Period'.

The question immediately leaps out at you: why did he measure from the centres of the pillars at each end, and not from the ends of the pillars at each end? Is that why his Third Period *loka* is so small? Fortunately he gives the measurements for each pillar, so we can add in 442.5 mm for the half width of pillar 'A' and 400 mm for the half width of pillar 'K'. This makes the overall length of the row of pillars as 49,300 mm. In fact, Posnansky did measure from the end of pillar 'A' to the end of pillar 'K' and found it to be 49 m

30 cm. But he then took the figure from the centre to the centre of the end pillars to use in his calculations instead!

Instead of dividing by 30 as Posnansky did on the assumption they represented periods of thirty days on a solar calendar, we can divide them by Egyptian royal cubits to see if there is any consistency with Egyptian royal cubits found previously at the Akapana pyramid. So 49,300 mm divided by 525 mm Egyptian royal cubit comes to 93.9 cubits, almost 94 cubits.

But the Egyptians had other variations in the length of the royal cubit, the cubit in which the Great Pyramid of Egypt is built has a length of 20.62 inches (523.74 mm) or sometimes quoted as 20.625 inches (523.87 mm) (see Berryman's *Historical Metrology*, pp. 71–2). This was the cubit used for land surveying and was derived from a *remen* which originated as a 1/5,000 part of the mean figure for a minute of latitude or geographic mile, where the *remen* formed the side of a square and the royal cubit was the diagonal of the square. Dividing the length of the pillars (49,300 mm) by 94 gives a cubit of 524.468 mm which is 20.64 inches, so it seems an 'Egyptian' royal cubit could after all have been intended. Berriman noted that when the King's Chamber of the Great Pyramid in Egypt was measured as accurately as possible by four different surveyors over a period of time, they each found a different length for the royal cubit ranging from 20.5 to 20.66 inches (showing how difficult it is to obtain a truly accurate measurement).

A further confirmation of the use of the royal cubits in Tiwanaku may be found in Posnansky's figure for the length of the terraces used to support the walls of the Kalasasaya which he measured as being 41 m 90 cm which would be 80 Egyptian royal cubits of 20.62 inches.

Posnansky seems to have considered the row of pillars as representing a calendar based upon thirty days and states that the solar year of twelve months was used with the Sun showing through the gap between the pillars each month. But there is a flaw with that. With eleven pillars, there are only ten gaps or spaces, not twelve. Posnansky would have done better to pay attention to one of his own quotes (section E, note 78) where he finds a sixteenth century Peruvian historian as saying: 'They divided the year into twelve months by the moons. Already each moon or month had its marker or pillar around Cuzco, where the sun arrived that month' (Ondegarda 1571).

The stone gateway which is today in the Kalasasaya is baptized 'the Gate of the Sun', and 'Kalasasaya' according to Posnansky simply means 'standing stones'. When he investigated Tiwanaku, the stone pillars had more of the appearance of a Stonehenge, there being no wall as there is today (most of the wall was assumed to have been carried off so in the 1960s as part of a reconstruction the spaces between the pillars were filled in to form a wall) and only ten of the giant pillars remained. The eleventh missing pillar may be found laying face down in a field some 229 metres to the west. According to Oscar Corvison, a Bolivian archeo-astronomer who studied the site, the eleven pillars represented the division of the year into periods of 20 (Corvison 1996). This seems more logical, since if you count from the central pillar (representing the equinox) out to the end pillar on the left (representing the south solstice), then back past the centre to the far right pillar (representing the north solstice), then back to the centre again, you arrive at a division of 20.

The Inca were sometimes said to be people of the sun, whereas the Aymara were said to be people of the moon, so I wonder whether in fact the pillars may also have been a soli-lunar calendar since what is called the 'Saros' cycle of lunar eclipses repeats itself every twenty 'Inca' years and twenty 'Inca years' of twelve months of 27.32 days is very close to eighteen solar years of 365.24 days (Allen 1998 and Aveni 2000). In addition, the people who built Tiwanaku were a race long before the Inca and possibly even before the Aymara.

On the other hand, if used for agricultural purposes, the temple may simply have marked the winter and summer solstices with the appropriate pillar or space between the pillars marking the return of the Sun to a suitable time for plantings crops, which is what Posnansky thought the purpose of the calendar was in the first place.

This is how it works. In the centre of the Kalasasaya, 30 *loka* (100 royal cubits) from the centre pillar, there is a large block of stone which is said to represent the original observation point. From here the Sun could be watched setting on the horizon over the pillars each night. When the Sun set over the central pillar, the day would be September 22 and spring would begin (the seasons being reversed in the southern hemisphere). When the Sun set over the next pillar to the left, one twentieth of a year would have passed and so on until, reaching the pillar at the far left a quarter of a year later on December 21, it now marked the summer solstice.

The Sun would now begin to move back towards the centre, reaching here another quarter of a year later on March 22, marking

Fig. 12.07. View of the Sun Gate with the calendar wall behind. The position of the missing pillar is marked by the arrow. Photo: Oscar Corvison.

the autumn equinox. Then it would continue to the right, reaching the end pillar on June 21, marking the winter solstice and the beginning of the Aymara New Year (the great festival of Inti Raymi). Returning back over the centre pillar one year later on the following September 22, the Sun would mark the beginning of another spring (explanation thanks to Oscar Corvison).

Although Corvison was correct in identifying the use of a solar calendar based on divisions of 20 (and this should not be a surprise since both the Aztec and Maya civilizations used a base 20 calendar), he does not seem to have considered the possibility it could also have been a lunar calendar.

However, on the above basis, when the Sun reached the first pillar it would have travelled a 1/20th of a year which is 18.26 days. By the time it reached midway to the next pillar, it would have travelled half as much again, which when added to the first figure means 27.39 days would have passed — virtually a sidereal lunar month. Every *one and a half* pillars would add another sidereal month and continuing the process this would take us back to the central pillar after thirteen and a third such sidereal lunar months (or divisions) had passed, completing a year and establishing a dual purpose, soli-lunar calendar.

Now I wondered if this in some way tied in with the Saros cycle and since it takes thirteen and a third siderial lunar months to circle round the calendar stones in order to complete one 'lap' and come back to a full year, how many 'laps' would it take to fulfil the Saros cycle?

Well, three 'laps' round the pillars would make the sun once more over the central pillar and represent forty sidereal lunar months and since each lap around the pillars is a solar year, a total of eighteen 'laps' round the pillars would complete the Saros cycle, the sun would be back again over the central pillar and the cycle would all begin all over again!

Maybe that's why the *amautas* (mathematicians) of the Aymara thought they had discovered the most perfect calendar in the world. Could this be the calendar of Atlantis? Some people thought so (Corvison 1996), but they failed to realize that the Altiplano *was* Atlantis.

The key to the calendar was said to be built into the Gate of the Sun, today found near the Kalasasaya pillar wall and put there when the Kalasasaya was restored. It consists of a giant block of stone with a gate cut into its lower half and an elaborate decoration on the upper part. In the centre of the decoration there is a representation of the 'weeping' god — presumably Viracocha — and in his hands he carries two staffs, which look like measuring or mathematical

Fig. 12.08. The frieze from the Sun Gate represents the eleven pillars on the calendar wall. Each pillar marks the position of the setting sun on a 1/20th of the Earth's orbit and a sidereal lunar month corresponds to the distance between one and a half pillars, representing 3/40ths of the orbit. Drawing by J.M. Allen after Oscar Corvison's interpretation of the vigesimal calendar system, with additional lunar interpretation by J.M. Allen.

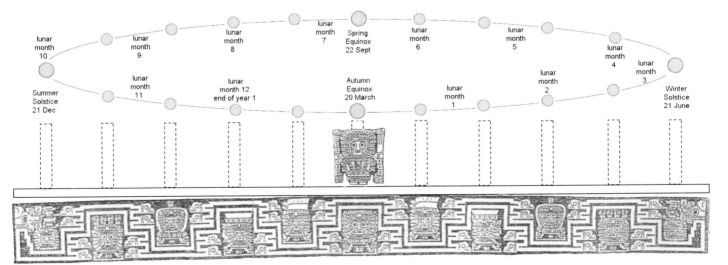

staffs since, although the rest of the monument is symmetrical, the staffs are different: the one in his right hand has two sets of three circles and the one in his left hand has two vertical lines over three circles. But who can read the monument today?

On the upper level, on each side there are three rows of iconic figures called *chasquis* — messengers of the gods. Each row has eight *chasquis,* but they are arranged with a block of five on the inner side and three on the outer side.

Beneath these *chasquis* there is a continuous row of smaller icons arranged so that eleven of them stand apart from the rest. We can assume that these eleven represent the pillars of the calendar. Now it has usually been wrongly assumed that because the upper *chasquis* in horizontal rows total fifteen on each side (not counting the outer ones) that the total of thirty *chasquis* represent thirty days since a solar year of 360 days divided by twelve months would give a thirty-day month. But, as explained above, the actual calendar is divided by twenty, which would make solar divisions of eighteen days, or three weeks of six days if used as a solar calendar.

Many people have mistakenly thought that the Gate of the Sun was the calendar, but it isn't. The pillar stones built into the west wall are the calendar and it could be instead, that the *chasquis* are telling you how to operate the calendar.

Instead of reading *horizontally*, if we read *vertically*, they seem to be saying, 'count in blocks of three'. But blocks of three what? When we studied the operation of the stones on the wall, we found that every one and a half pillars represented one sidereal lunar month. Therefore every half division between the pillars represented one fortieth of the year or a third of a sidereal lunar month, the month itself being the prime unit. Now on the Gate of the Sun there are a total of 48 *chasqui* icons which therefore represent 48 sidereal lunar months. Tahuantinsuyo, the empire of the Incas, was 'the land of the four quarters, or four divisions' so dividing the 48 *chasquis* by 4 results in twelve *chasquis* — meaning twelve sidereal lunar months — which was the Inca lunar year of 328 days. In turn 328 days divided by 4 gave the 82-day period at the end of which the Moon would be visible against the same group of stars, and that, I believe, is the message of the *chasquis* — how to operate the calendar.

Posnansky also measured an inner temple he calls the 'Sanctissimum' in the centre of the Kalasasaya complex and found it to measure 63.80 × 71.80 metres. Had he measured it in sacred cubits of 25 inches, he might have defined the same measurements as 100 × 113 sacred cubits.

Fig. 12.09. Recently uncovered steps at the pyramid of Akapana, Tiwanaku.

Fig. 12.10. Recently uncovered terraces at the pyramid of Akapana, Tiwanaku.

Pre-Egyptians and ancient South America

In the 'Old World' the confusion of so many different measuring units led to the introduction of the metre in 1790, which was intended by the French Academy of Sciences to be a new decimal system based upon a division of the Earth's quadrant circumference — the distance from the North Pole to the Equator — into 10,000,000 parts. The originators of the modern metre were completely unaware that a 'metric' unit already existed in ancient Egypt where the royal cubit of 525 mm was then divided into 28 digits, while 24 digits gave the cubit of 450 mm, and 16 digits gave the 'metric' foot of 300 mm (Tompkins 1978).

Amongst the other values of Egyptian cubit, the cubit used for land surveying of 20.625 inches (523.87 mm), was also related mathematically to the Sumerian cubit of 19.8 inches (30 *shusi*) in the ratio of 24/25 and it is no surprise that the 'Sumerian 'yard' of 33.0 inches has also been found in Peru. So when we say the sides of the Akapana pyramid have a measurement in Egyptian Royal Cubits we could also put it the alternative way round, as John Villegas pointed out: 'Or is it that the Egyptian pyramids are built in "Bolivian cubits"!'

At the same time though, we cannot discount the fact that different cultures could arrive at the same value for their cubits because they both used as a starting point the dimensions of the Earth subdivided according to their own mathematical preferences.

Colonel A. Braghine had something to say about the 'pre-Egyptians' in his book *The Shadow of Atlantis*:

> Later M. Frot wrote me a very interesting letter, which I give below in a brief English translation: 'The Phoenicians used in their South American inscriptions the same methods which were used by the old Egyptians at the earliest period of hieroglyphic writing. The same methods were employed by the Aztecs and by that unknown race which has left its petroglyphs in the Amazonian basin. The results of my investigations are so striking that I am afraid to publish them. In order to give you an idea of them I will say only that I possess proofs of the origins of Egyptians: the forefathers of Egyptians issued from South America and once formed three

powerful empires. Two of them were founded in South America and the third on the old Continent. The latter included north-western Africa, the Iberian Peninsula and the islands of the ocean neighbouring Europe. The pre-Egyptians started their migration eastwards from the point at 57° 42' 45' West longitude from Greenwich (Frot does not give the latitude at this point) and this event is mentioned in an old Toltec document which I possess and which, besides the above information, contains also a short history of the pre-Egyptians. Moreover, I have discovered in Amazonia an inscription which contains an account of the voyage of a certain pre-Egyptian priest to what is now Bolivia'. The last words of this interesting letter from M. Frot apparently concern a discovery in the basin of the Río Madeira, an inscription much discussed at that time in the Brazilian press. The deciphering of it established that at some remote period a group of pre-Egyptians moved to the Bolivian silver mines. (Braghine 1980)

What is particularly interesting about this statement regarding the 'pre-Egyptians' is the location of their starting point: '57° 42' 45' West longitude from Greenwich'. In my earlier work *Atlantis: the Andes Solution,* I hinted that the famous lost city of Tarshish was located on an island near Asunción and followed this up in *The Atlantis Trail* with an antique map showing the actual island in the entrance to the Pilcomayo River (see Figs. 12.11 and 12.12). This map was seen on the wall of a government office in Bolivia and clearly showed an island in the entrance to the Pilcomayo.

The Pilcomayo is the river which was called the 'River of Silver' and led to the Silver Mountain at Potosi, and was also a route which could be followed to Atlantis and the Altiplano.

Although Braghine does not give the latitude of his source's 'starting point' for the pre-Egyptians, what is certain is that his line of longitude 57° 42' 45' West, passes exactly through this island in the entrance to the Pilcomayo River. This would confirm that it was most probably the seaport for Atlantis and the site of Tarshish from which the great fleets sailed for the port of Gebel on the Gulf of Aqaba, taking the precious metals from there overland to become part of the treasure of Solomon's Temple.

Fig. 12.11. and 12.12. Antique map showing island at the entrance to the Pilcomayo.

Fig. 12.13. One of the sculptures to be seen in the Tiwanaku museum. Plato said, 'there was something outlandish about their appearance', and I think he got it fairly right! There is something also 'Egyptian' about their appearance, and note the turban this one is wearing!

Satellite images today show this area to be heavily urbanized with islands at the entrance in a different position probably due to deposits of mud and silt washed down by the river. Today the river Pilcamayo is no longer navigable from its entrance at the river Paraguay to the foothills of the Andes, but the important thing to remember is that it is a route which could be followed like a signpost pointing the way to the Silver Mountain at Potosi and thence to the level Altiplano and the former city of Atlantis.

The existence of a city on an island in the river Pilcomayo is confirmed by an old Spanish chronicle written by Juan de Santa Cruz Pachacuti Yanqui Salcamaygua *(Cronica relazion de antigua-dades de este reino del Piru, 1603).*

This account refers to a great city on an island in the Pilcomayo, not at its lower entrance in the río Paraguay, but higher up the river not far from Tarija. Closer to the foothills of the Andes, it is at the junction of the río Pilcomayo and the río Pilaya, which is particularly interesting since both rivers rise in the silver mountain of Potosi. The Pilcomayo continues on past the silver mountain on its northern side to its origins near Challapata and the peak known as Asanaque, while the Pilaya approaches Potosi from the south and has its origin in the silver mountain.

So a city at the junction of these two rivers is again an ideal site for a city whose main industry was the collection and exportation of precious metals, while the lower site near the río Paraguay would have been more suitable for larger vessels which could not travel so far inland.

Since many people have misquoted me by suggesting that Atlantis on Lake Poopó or even Titicaca, which it has sometimes been confused with, had a direct outlet to the Pacific or Atlantic Oceans, I have to clarify that within Plato's timescale, the Andes are assumed to have always been at their present altitude. So the canal to the sea was a canal to the inland sea previously described, not a canal from Atlantis to the Atlantic or Pacific Oceans. Therefore porters would be necessary to transport any goods from the high altitudes to the lower levels, and vice versa.

This is clearly illustrated in a sixteenth century engraving which shows porters dragging canoes overland from an unknown river to an inland salt lake on which sat the fabulous city of Manoa, otherwise known as *El Dorado* (see Fig. 12.15).

The situation is similar to that of the headwaters of the river Pilcomayo relative to that of Lake Poopó, and in the drawing the saltwater lake is named as Lake Parime.

The original name of Lake Poopó was Lake Aullagas, a corruption from the Uru name 'Ullakjasa'. Lake Poopó or Pupu comes from the Quechua and has been variously known by other names such as Pazna or *Paria,* not too different from the 'Parime' mentioned above.

And with its golden walls and temples, it is not unreasonable to suppose that it may have been Atlantis itself, built on an island on the inland salt sea of Lake Poopó, which may also have been the source of the El Dorado legend.

Fig. 12.14 Outside the church at Tiwanaku are to be found two monoliths similar to those inside the Tiwanaku museum. Although badly eroded by weather and time, the intriguing question is the question of the head-dress which seems to show a representation of a snake coiled around it — and a snake on a head-dress was the symbol of ancient Egypt!

Fig. 12.15. 'The Search for El Dorado', a sixteenth century engraving showing porters dragging canoes overland from an unknown river to an inland salt lake on which was built the city of El Dorado. Illustration courtesy of Time-Life Books.

13. The Dating Question

As we have seen, the date of Plato's Atlantis has always been a problem. Atlantis is usually assumed to have existed some nine thousand years before Solon, the Greek statesman who lived around 600 BC and who brought back the story from Egypt. Plato gave a date of around 9600 BC whilst at the same time describing a Bronze Age civilization. The usual comment is that there were no civilizations anywhere in the world at that time, and no one around to record and hand down the story either.

That is to say, there were no known civilizations in Greece or Egypt at that time, but if a civilization had existed on the Altiplano and been destroyed in the great cataclysm Plato described, then survivors could have existed on the South American continent.

First of all Plato tells us that eight thousand years was the duration of the Egyptian civilization, and the Athenian civilization was founded earlier by the space of one thousand years. But we have to note that he does not actually give the date for the founding of Atlantis — we assume it was contemporary with the founding of Athens —and so, in that case, he gave the same date for the founding of Athens/Atlantis as he gave for the destruction of Atlantis, that is, nine thousand years before Solon.

That is the same date when the waters of Lake Coipasa dried up and so could have represented a propitious time for the 'founding' of Atlantis as a civilization on the Altiplano.

So, in his own words, Plato is 'recounting the tale of the citizens who lived nine thousand years previously' and then goes on to tell us quite plainly, 'nine thousand is the sum of years since the war occurred' and talks about a war between a confederation of nations which invaded Greece and Egypt and how the Athenian forces defeated the invaders — 'the Athenian State was the bravest in war and supremely well organized in other respects'.

Plato wanted to record 'the finest of the achievements of the Greeks' — in fact he gives the same number of ships for the fleet of Atlantis as Homer did for the Greek fleet against Troy suggesting that this part of the story was based upon Homer. If, as we saw earlier, we substitute lunar months for years in Plato's account then the 'nine thousand years' before Solon becomes nine thousand months before Solon, or 1263 BC — the date of the Trojan war which is also roughly consistent with the period for the founding of Athens by Theseus in 1400 bc.

In fact, this date is borne out by the statement of Pedro Sarmiento de Gamboa which specifically mentions *nine thousand lunar months* and specifically names 1320 BC for the actual event by his own calculation.

The 'confederated nations' which Plato called 'Atlantis' and which he said attacked Egypt and Greece and attempted to enslave all of the eastern Mediterranean, would therefore be the 'Sea Peoples', a confederation of nations which invaded Egypt both by land and by sea in the years around 1220 BC and 1186 bc.

We might go as far as to say that the first part of the story, the geographic description of the region of Atlantis, is clearly the Altiplano on the continent of 'South America'. Given the fact that Pampa Aullagas island is covered in coral-like *katawi* which dates to the waters of the early lakes Tauca and Coipasa, we cannot rule out the possibility that an early civilization existed here which was overwhelmed by the waters of Lake Coipasa in 11,000 BC — this being consistent also with a climate six degrees warmer, the presence of mastodons and the absence of salt salars since the plain would have been covered with fertile mud from the earlier lake. But it seems equally possible that after the waters dried up in 9500 bc, Atlantis existed in one of the periods when the Altiplano had varying water levels due to the climatic changes — we should note the starting date for the Aymara calendar dates to 3507 BC — suggesting that a bronze age Atlantis contemporary with the Sea Peoples may have flourished from this date to its demise around 1200 bc. Perhaps like Troy, there have been several cities or cultures on the same site, confirmed by the fact that the site is still occupied today and covered in numerous terraces and platforms dating to the Inca/ Aymara re-occupation.

A traveller's tale of Atlantis

Imagine you are an Egyptian priest listening to a traveller giving an account of where he came from — and for this, I will use the words of Plato, so here is the story as a person arriving from Atlantis/ South America might have told it:

> First of all I live on a continent the size of North
> Africa and Asia combined. It is located in the Atlantic
> Ocean opposite the Pillars of Hercules. In the centre
> of the continent, next to the sea and midway along

the longest side of the continent there is a plain. This plain is completely level, it is of rectangular shape and elongated and is enclosed by mountains. It is high above the level of the ocean. In the mountains there are many streams and villages also a great number of mastodons. There are many mines including gold, silver, tin, copper and the second most valuable metal — orichalcum — called tumbaga in our language and which is a natural alloy of copper and gold. When the surface is polished the copper dissolves out and the gold remains giving a sparkling surface.

But the part where I live was formerly the capital of the whole country. It is a volcanic island located in the centre of the plain and five miles from the sea.

It was originally the home of the god of rivers and watercourses, a friend to humankind called in some parts of our country, Tunupa and in others, Viracocha, or in Greek as you say, Poseidon. Our god in female form married a god called Azanaques who lived on a hill, just as in Greek, Poseidon married Cleito, and had four pairs of twin offspring — although some, including the Greeks, recount five pairs.

This was before ships and sailing were invented and the God took hold of the island and made it impregnable to man, with alternating zones of land and sea, enclosing each other like concentric circles.

The whole of the island was enclosed with a wall of stone and the stones were of the most beautiful colours, black, red and white. In the centre of the island was a temple sacred to the God and plated with gold, silver and orichalcum.

Around the perimeter of the level plain ran a giant canal which collected the streams from the mountains and discharged them into the sea in the vicinity of the city, and across the plain were dug numerous smaller canals and the land was cropped twice a year.

A fountain of water sprang forth from the central island and this was conducted to the outer groves where there were many plantations for the soil was most fertile.

The people lived there for many generations but in the end their greed for material possessions overwhelmed them so Kjuni (Zeus as they say in Greek), god of the sky and thunderbolts and king of the gods, decided to punish them and in the end the city was swallowed up and disappeared into the sea.

So here the reader can see that the description of Atlantis is merely a geographic description of the continent opposite the Strait of Gibraltar — now called South America — and the level rectangular plain which exists in the centre of this continent. When it was first discovered by the Europeans it was correctly identified as Atlantis, but when it was later given the name 'America' after Amerigo Vespucci its true name became lost forever.

And the island described above is the island of Cerro Santos Villca at the village of Pampa Aullagas on the southern shore of Lake Poopó.

Anyone visiting the island will see that it has been destroyed by the earthquakes mentioned above and is still covered in white, sedimentary lake deposits from the time when the lake was at a higher level.

Behind the village of Pampa Aullagas they will see the remains of an outer ring of land with a gap between for the ships to sail through — exactly as Plato described it. They will also see the wall of stone enclosing the island, the black, red and white stones and the site has been inhabited for a long time by successive cultures. It has a natural source of water as mentioned above and the water is still conducted by channels to concentric cultivated plots.

14. Postscript

Just as no letter is complete without a postscript, equally so a book of this nature would not be complete without a postscript. This is due to the nature of the work itself, which, unlike a novel, which may exist pre-written in the mind of the author, or be made up as the author goes along, has developed into a programme of research which has spread over several years and each visit to Bolivia has revealed a little piece more in the puzzle of Atlantis.

In fact, it has become a project as much as a book. In the beginning, that is, in the days before the Internet, there was little information available about South America. Only a very few books in the local public library and each Landsat photo had to be bought and paid for and they were very expensive.

So the first booklet which was self-published and ran to a mere thirty pages was published in 1982 and had a very limited distribution — the great pitfall of most self-publishing endeavours.

Then after being invited by Colonel John Blashford-Snell to participate with him in a BBC radio interview, I had an offer from a small publishing firm, Windrush Press, to publish the first book, *Atlantis: the Andes Solution,* which appeared in 1998.

By the year 2000, when we were filming in Bolivia for the Discovery documentary 'Atlantis in the Andes', or certainly by 2001 when the documentary was released, the book had gone out of print and Windrush Press had been taken over by a large publishing conglomerate Orion who expressed no interest in continuing it.

That is a familiar pattern these days when it is virtually impossible for an unknown or little known author to be published and the many small publishing houses have all been bought up by publishing giants who operate using the names of the original smaller companies as 'imprints'.

So *Atlantis: the Andes Solution,* became the first book in what was to become a trilogy, offering the public the theory of Atlantis on the Altiplano in South America.

This was followed in 2001 by book two, *The Atlantis Trail* (published in Bolivia as *La Ruta de la Atlántida*) which was a record of the various expeditions around the Altiplano before finding the site at Pampa Aullagas.

By 2006 I had completed book three, *Atlantis: Lost Kingdom of the Andes,* which was meant to show what we had actually found on the site itself, and which was intended to be the final book in the trilogy.

But then high resolution satellite images became available online, which showed numerous parallel canals around Oruro, so these had to be added to the book, and so the work continues because literally, 'there is always something new to discover in Bolivia!'

And contrary to most of the press and tourist guide books, the Altiplano is not a 'cold and unhospitable place' — well, maybe in June and July it is somewhat cold, as the European summer coincides with the Andean winter. But I have always gone there at most other times of the year, when I have found the place and the people warm and friendly, and the Altiplano itself incredibly beautiful, even more so in the more remote areas.

And now, as a result of the various expeditions, the people living in the villages have been keen to participate in a development of the area as a future tourist destination, and in 2006 a law was passed in the Congress of Bolivia to support them in this purpose.

It is hoped that this will lead to the building of a tarmaced road leading around Lake Poopó to the Atlantis village at Pampa Aullagas and then continuing on to the Salar de Uyuni from where jeeps can cross the salt flat to Uyuni, an already popular tourist destination, although the real 'Atlantis Trail', runs not across the Salar de Uyuni, but across and around the Salar de Coipasa, all within the territory of Oruro.

The latest satellite evidence

But the main motivation for writing a postscript is to include more satellite photos and reflections on the subject of canals, mines and mountain routes to the sea. That is because the canals were key features in Plato's story of Atlantis and the system of alternating drought and flooding are features of the Altiplano which continue to this day. Also while I was looking on satellite images for routes through the mountains, the extent of the mining and proximity of the mines to Lake Poopó became more apparent.

I have already mentioned how, back in 1983 when I first bought some Landsat pictures, I thought I could see evidence of canals running across them but how all the experts laughed at the idea of canals running across the Altiplano.

Then, with the help of the Internet and the public release of high resolution satellite images, it can be seen from the latest satellite evidence — and some of these images are shown earlier (Figs 7.05 to 7.11) in this book — how the area around Oruro which today is mostly sparsely populated salt desert, is covered in old canals and abandoned cultivations.

Some of these channels running for long distances in perfectly straight lines are more recent attempts to provide relief drainage and also serve the dual purpose of aiding irrigation; some are reported to have been dug in the 1950's, but the sheer quantity of these channels which run through the salt flats and even under the present day rivers suggest the vast majority must have a much greater antiquity. They certainly prove that what Plato said was eminently possible in this area.

Yet, here is a typical comment found on the Internet only recently and dating from the year 2004, but referring to the time around the year 2000 when we were making the Discovery film. It is based on an interview between Carl Zimmer, who writes books and articles about science and whom the *New York Times Book Review* calls 'as fine a science essayist as we have' and Simon Lamb who had just had published a book about geology in the Andes.

> Simon Lamb, a geologist at Oxford University, got a call one day from a television producer about pictures of Atlantis. The lost civilization could be found on 12,000 ft high plains nestled in the Andes Mountains. An Atlantis expert (whatever that is) had shown the producer satellite photographs of the plains, pointing out canals running in parallel straight lines for miles. What more proof could one ask for? The producer called Lamb, an expert on the Andes, for confirmation.
>
> Lamb pulled out his own satellite photographs, found the canals, and laughed. He told the producer that canals had formed naturally, without any help from Atlanteans. Hundreds of millions of years ago, before the Andes existed, rocks had slowly piled up in layers. Later the rocks were heaved onto their side and raised up thousands of feet, whereupon rain began to flow down their exposed flanks. The water gnawed away at the weakest layers, creating a series of straight-edged channels. As he spoke, Lamb could sense hostility on the other end of the line. The producer didn't want to hear about strata and erosion.

'Well, that's your explanation, anyway,'he huffed,
and went off to make his documentary without
Lamb's help. 'Atlantis in the Andes' later appeared on
the Learning Channel.

This story has a silver lining. The conversation
inspired Lamb to demonstrate just how fascinating
the Atlantis-free Andes are. The result is *Devil in the
Mountain,* an absorbing account of the many years
Lamb has spent exploring and pondering the Andes.

The above shows the typical type of hostility to the notion that
any system of irrigation canals could have existed on the Altiplano
or that any advanced culture could have existed there to have created
it, and especially if that culture should dare to be called Atlantis.

The major problem facing archaeology in Bolivia is lack of
funding. There are so many potential sites and the Bolivians themselves have had little money to dedicate to archaeology, so they
have had to rely for research programmes on a few expeditions
from American or European institutions.

Satellite images continue to reveal potential sites for investigation and if the true resources of satellite technology were dedicated
to this end, it might lead to startling results.

Sometimes images can be misleading, especially the smaller
Landsat images that were the only ones available a few years ago.
I remember very well having discovered a circular formation to the
north west of Oruro and taking a BBC film crew there at the time
of the Kota Mama expeditions around 1998.

It turned out to be the large circular slurry tank for the gold mining operation at La Joya. Not wishing to go home empty handed,
they filmed it anyway, which later cast a somewhat negative aspect
on the film and shows the amount of background research that has
to be done and the advantage of doing a 'recce' before taking film
crews with you!

Years later, and again thanks to the Internet, I realize the significance of the mine at La Joya. It is the largest gold mine in Bolivia
and located on the River Desaguadero to the north west of Oruro.
In Spanish, *La Joya* means 'the jewel' but in the original Aymara
language, the name is *La Khoya* which means 'the mine'.

Satellite images have been useful for following the routes of the
rivers and valleys leading from the high level Altiplano to the lower
levels and hence the Atlantic Ocean.

Opposite Pampa Aullagas on the eastern side of the lake there is the village of Challapata and just above this a river drains into a small lake and thence into Lake Poopó. Following this river a short distance upstream one comes to its source then following the route of the valley one comes to another tiny lake which is the origin of a river flowing in the opposite direction; this river becomes in turn the Río Aguas Calientes (river of hot waters) then the River Pilcomayo. One tributary leads directly to the silver mountain at Potosi and another emerges at Asunción in Paraguay with access to the Atlantic Ocean at Buenos Aires.

To the north-east of Tarija, the River Pilcomayo is joined by the River Pilaya. This river runs westwards, one branch providing a southerly approach to the silver mountain at Potosi, another branch passes through Tupiza and provides an access route to the south east corner of the Altiplano at Uyuni, with one branch leading directly to the mining complex at Minas Animas.

Oruro itself has some of the oldest mining tunnels in Bolivia, running beneath the mountain in what became the San José mine, a source of silver and tin, and yet another source of tin, the largest tin mine in Bolivia, exists at Huanuni, in a valley a short distance to the south east of Oruro. Near here also are the famous tin mining complexes at Llallagua, Catavi, and Uncia, and this river which passes Llallagua and Catavi eventually opens into the Río Grande which discharges via the Amazon into the Atlantic Ocean. The importance of tin being that when combined with copper it created bronze, a valuable metal for the ancients and, equally, at the time of Simon Patiño, the Bolivian tin baron who developed the industry there. At the turn of the twentieth century, it had become a valuable metal of the future with the invention of the tin can, so much so, that on discovering his mountain, Simon Patiño prayed, 'Let it be tin, not silver!'

To the south of Pampa Aullagas/Atlantis exists another river, the River Marquez which a short distance upstream leads to the village of Urukilla. And here was another mine, a mine of orichalcum, the naturally occurring gold/copper alloy of Plato.

Urukilla was also the original home of the present villagers of Pampa Aullagas who in the sixteenth century were rounded up by the Spanish *conquistadores* from their scattered hamlets and settled in small towns, the origin of the present village of Pampa Aullagas and no doubt contributing to the loss of their original identity and knowledge of their own original history.

The point is, all around the lake and all around the original site of Atlantis are the richest mines in the world providing all the valu-

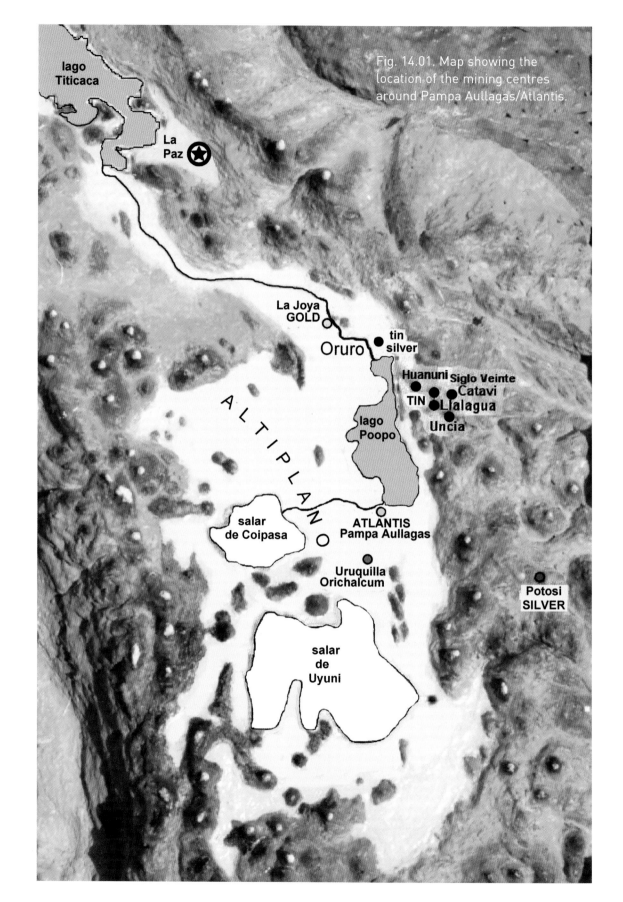

Fig. 14.01. Map showing the location of the mining centres around Pampa Aullagas/Atlantis.

able metals mentioned by Plato, gold, silver, tin and orichalcum and in the days before jeeps and modern roads, the rivers and their tributaries were routes that could be followed by canoe and on foot to arrive at these valuable mines.

While I was tracing these rivers by high-resolution satellite images and looking for a route where one could cross from the valley leading up past Huanuni and into the valley leading down from Llallagua and the Río Grande, a curious circular formation on the ground caught my attention.

It looked like the remains of a circular ditch then further across the images were what looked like small sections of old tracks which could have been around 20ft (6 metres) wide and could be followed for a distance of around six miles (10 km). That is to say, the sections were like pieces in a jigsaw puzzle since they were few and far between and in the gaps between them, there was nothing whatsoever remaining on the ground.

At first the circular ditch reminded me of a possible turning circle for a railway, but I could see no sign of a railway track yet the route seemed to have followed the contours of the mountains, much in the way a railway might have.

Simon Patiño built a railway from Machacamarca right up to Uncia, near his mines at Catavi and Llallagua and this was completed in 1921, but this railway could be seen on the other side of the valley. Similarly, an ancient road would not have followed so neatly the contours of the mountains, nor have had such wonderful curves, nor have been engineered to gradually decrease the gradient.

And what was the purpose of this circle which seemed to lead to nowhere? The answer is that it was not just a circle sitting there on its own without purpose. It only appeared that way because it was part of a route most of which had been destroyed by earthquakes. If one studied the route closely, one could see where it had been engineered to turn gently around in the circle then head back south again, but at a lower level, then it had entered another turning circle, now destroyed by earthquakes and headed yet again north once more at a lower level, again with much of the route destroyed by earthquakes (see Fig. 14.02).

As I was always on the lookout for remains of old canals, an alternative explanation seemed that it might have been part of a mountain canal, perhaps engineered to water the agricultural terraces, the remains of which could also be seen nearby, some turned around, twisted and distorted by earthquakes. Or if a former part of the railway, it seems almost unbelievable that a section of railway

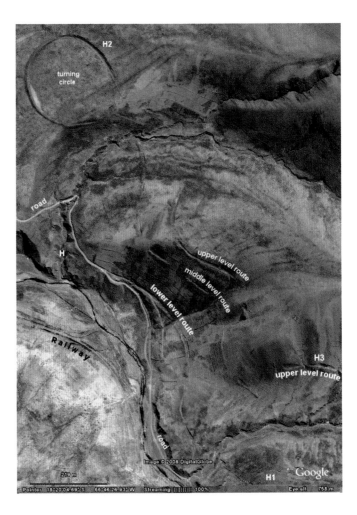

Fig. 14.02. On this photo can be seen the route at three different altitude levels. Crossing the mountains and entering from H3 it ran to the turning circle at H2 (746 ft or 227 metres in diameter) then headed south at a middle level passing H1 before turning again via another circle of similar size, now disappeared, and heading north at a lower level, crossing the ravine at H to disappear at the western edge of the photo.

built in the 1920s could have so completely disappeared. Like many other details, this awaits future expeditions to provide the definitive answer and the satellite images remain as always, useful starting points for future investigations. In fact, it was the satellite images that drew my attention to the concentration of mining in this area in the first place, since although I had heard of the tin and silver mines in this region, and particularly Catavi, I didn't really know where they were until coming across them on the satellite images on my search for river routes.

It is clear that much of the area has been completely destroyed in some great earthquake upheaval, many of the walled terraces are no longer where they were originally because of landslip and many of them obliterated completely. But then weren't earthquakes and cataclysm so much a part of Plato's story!

Fig. 14.03. Satellite technology measures the length of the line, that is, the width of the Paria canal, as 200 ft with embankments 25 ft wide. Source: Google Earth.

This route, or the little that is left of it, shows the devastation that earthquakes cause, and also illustrates why it is so difficult to find evidence of the Atlantis civilization in the region.

The large canal, one stade wide, which Plato described seems similarly for the majority to have disappeared although a one stade wide section of channel remains to the west of Lake Poopó and joins a series of underground wells much as the way the smaller channels around Oruro seem to.

As mentioned earlier, the satellite imagery is certainly useful for pinpointing features for further investigation and satellite images again show two more sections of what looks like giant canal, firstly to the west of Paria (just north of Oruro) where it measures 200 ft between embankments and 250 ft to the outside of the embankments. Another section of similar canal of identical size and construction discharges the Río Desaguadero into Lake UruUru just south of Oruro.

Without ground observation it is impossible to tell whether such features are indeed ancient or perhaps the result of more recent activities such as mining or as has been suggested for the Paria section, a means of supplying domestic water to Oruro, though no actual purpose can be seen on the satellite images and the ruinous condition suggests they have been there a long time.

The satellite can reveal features not easily seen on the ground and the ruinous state of the Paria canal shows how even large con- structions like this can be washed away leaving hardly a trace of their previous extent and purpose.

They are certainly of dimensions compatible with those huge canals of Plato and give the reader a comparison of size, bearing in mind the phrase of Plato, 'it seems incredible that they should be so large as the account states, given that they were made by hand and in addition to all the other operations but we must report what we heard, the width was one stade'.

Fig. 14.04. Oblique view showing the 200 ft wide channel at Paria looking from West to East. Source: Google Earth.

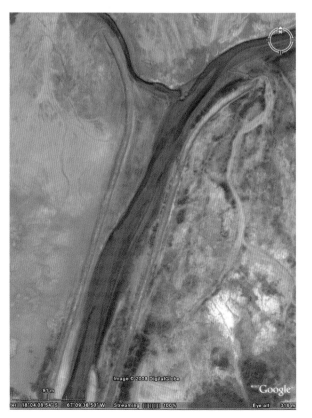

Fig. 14.05. Satellite image showing northern end of the 200 ft canal which today discharges the river Desaguadero into Lake UruUru. Source: Google Earth.

Appendix A:

Comparative table of locations/attributes needed for site of Atlantis, based on Milos Atlantis Conference criteria, 2005

In July, 2005, the Milos Atlantis Conference held in Greece ('The Atlantis Hypothesis: Searching for a Lost Land'), listed twenty-four criteria to qualify a site where Atlantis could have existed. A summary of the results is given below for each proposed site. Some of these are not provable due to lack of data, but Bolivia meets twenty of these criteria plus a further ten listed below, making a total of thirty out of thirty-four.

List of Criteria against proposed sites	Bolivia	Thera	Troy	Andalucia	Azores	Cuba	Antarctica
1. The Metropolis of Atlantis should have been located where an island used to be and where parts of it may still exist.	yes	yes	yes	no	no	no	no
2. The Metropolis of Atlantis should have had a most distinct geomorphology composed of alternating concentric rings of land and water.	yes	no	no	no	no	no	no
3. Atlantis was located outside the Pillars of Hercules (at a distant point in the Atlantic Ocean).	yes	no	no	no	yes	yes	yes
4. Atlantis was larger than Libya and Asia combined (meaning northern Africa and the Middle East).	yes	no	no	no	no	no	yes
5. On a low hill about 50 stades inland within the capital city itself, an inner citadel was erected to protect the original home of Cleito and Poseidon (the city was 50 stadia from the sea).	yes	no	no	no	no	no	no
6. Atlantis had hot and cold-water springs, with mineral deposits (essentially including gold, silver, tin, orichalcum).	yes	no	no	yes	no	no	no
7. Atlantis had red, white and black rocks.	yes	yes	no	no	yes	no	no
8. Atlantis sheltered a wealthy population with literate, building, mining, metallurgical and navigational skills.	yes	yes	yes	yes	no	no	no

List of Criteria against proposed sites	Bolivia	Thera	Troy	Andalucia	Azores	Cuba	Antarctica
9. The main region of Atlantis lay on a coastal plain, measuring 2,000 × 3,000 stades, surrounded by mountains which rose precipitously high above sea level.	yes	no	no	no	no	no	no
10. Atlantis faced south and was sheltered from the northern winds (as on mountain at Pampa Aullagas).	yes	no	no	no	no	no	no
11. The Atlanteans had created a checkerboard pattern of canals for irrigation.	yes	no	no	no	no	no	no
12. Atlantis had a rich spectrum of wild and domesticated flora and fauna, including elephants.	yes	no	no	no	no	no	no
13. Atlantis had a high population density, enough to support a large army composed of 1,200,000 men, 10,000 chariots and 1,200 ships.	yes	no	no	no	no	no	no
14. Atlantis controlled Libya up to the borders of Egypt and Europe as far as Tyrrhenia (Tuscany).							
15. The religion of Atlantis involved the sacrifice of bulls (in Bolivia, llama sacrifice is common).	yes	yes	no	yes	no	no	no
16.The kings of Atlantis assembled alternatively every fifth and sixth year.							
17. The Metropolis of Atlantis must have suffered a devastating physical destruction of unprecedented proportions.	yes	yes	no	no	no	no	no
18. Earthquakes and floods of extraordinary violence were the precursors of Atlantis' destruction.	yes	yes	no	no	no	no	no
19. The Metropolis of Atlantis was swallowed by the sea and vanished under the water, following the occurrence of earthquakes and floods.	yes	yes	no	no	no	no	no
20. At the time of its destruction, Atlantis was at war with Athens.							
21. Atlantis should have been reachable from Athens by sea.	yes	yes	yes	yes	yes	yes	no
22. After the destruction of Atlantis, the passage of ships was blocked by shallows due to mud just below the surface, the remains of the sunken island.	yes	no	no	no	no	no	no

List of Criteria against proposed sites	Bolivia	Thera	Troy	Andalucia	Azores	Cuba	Antarctica
23. The Metropolis of Atlantis was destroyed nine thousand years before the sixth century BC.							
24. No physically or geologically impossible processes were involved in the formation and destruction of the Metropolis of Atlantis, but could not have been responsible for the destruction of a landmass the size of a continent. Also, no physically or geologically impossible processes were involved in the formation of hot water springs and in the formation of red, white and black rocks.	yes	yes	no	no	no	no	no
	20	**9**	**2**	**4**	**3**	**2**	**2**
25. 'the continent was the way to other islands and the continent beyond ...' (meaning Asia).	yes	no	no	no	no	no	no
26. 'the plain was in the centre of the island mid-way along its longest side ...' (Lee's translation).	yes	no	no	no	no	no	no
27. 'the plain was high above the level of the sea ...' (meaning the ocean)	yes	no	no	no	no	no	no
28. 'the plain had a smooth and level surface ...'	yes	no	no	no	no	no	no
29. 'they raised two crops per year ...' (due to a system of raised fields with water channels).	yes	no	no	no	no	no	no
30. 'the wealth they possessed was so great that the like will never easily be seen again ...'	yes	no	no	no	no	no	no
31. 'they made statues in gold of their ancestors ...' (this was customary in Peru)	yes	no	no	no	no	no	no
32. 'there were mines of orichalcum' (naturally ocurring deposits and mines of orichalcum exist in Bolivia).	yes	no	no	no	no	no	no
33. 'five pairs of twin sons' (also occurs in Inca legend).	yes	no	no	no	no	no	no
34. origin of the name 'Atl' and 'Antis' (these are words of South American origin).	yes	no	no	no	no	no	no
	30	**9**	**2**	**4**	**3**	**2**	**2**

Appendix B:

Fifty Point Comparison between Atlantis and the Altiplano

Below follows a comparison of the main points of Plato's geographic description of Atlantis, in relation to the Altiplano in Bolivia next to Lake Poopó.

The bulk of the translation in the tables is that of Benjamin Jowett (1892). In some places, I have added the translations by R.G. Bury (1929) and Sir Desmond Lee (1971) in order to amplify the original text.

From the Timaeus	**Interpretation and comments**
Then listen, Socrates, to a tale which, though strange, is certainly true. And what is this ancient famous action of the Athenians, which Critias declared, on the authority of Solon, to be not a mere legend, but an actual fact? And what other, Critias, can we find that will be better than this, which is natural and suitable to the festival of the goddess, and has the very great advantage of being a fact and not a fiction?	Plato says three times that the Atlantis story is a true story. He says that they are going to use this story as the basis of a story which they will use and build upon at the festival of Athena.
You must not be surprised if you should perhaps hear Hellenic names given to foreigners, Solon, who was intending to use the tale for his poem, enquired into the meaning of the names, and found that the early Egyptians in writing them down had translated them into their own language ... And he recovered the meaning of the several names and when copying them out again translated them into our language ...	Poseidon was the Greek god of the sea, known as Neptune in Rome and Tunupa, Viracocha or Pachacamac in Bolivia. Other words such as *trireme* is the familiar Greek name for a ship or warship and *hoplite* a Greek soldier.
The goddess Athene or Neith in the Egyptian tongue ... founded your city a thousand years before ours, and afterwards she founded ours, of which the constitution is recorded in our sacred registers to be eight thousand years old.	According to the tale, Egypt was founded around 8600 BC and Athens in 9600 BC.

As touching your citizens of nine thousand years ago ...	There is no record of civilizations in Egypt or Greece in 9600 BC, but Plato uses the same date for the destruction of Atlantis as he does for the founding of Athens and the wars between Atlantis, Athens and Egypt.
1. For these histories tell of a mighty power which unprovoked made an expedition against the whole of Europe and Asia. This power came forth out of the Atlantic Ocean ... (Jowett) For it is related in our records how once upon a time your state stayed the course of a mighty host, which, starting from a distant point in the Atlantic ocean ... (Bury) Our records tell how your city checked a great power which arrogantly advanced from its base in the Atlantic ocean ... (Lee)	Atlantis was located in the Atlantic Ocean. It is pointless to try and relocate Atlantis to within the Straits or move the Straits to inside the Mediterranean, because the text clearly says Atlantis was a continent in the Atlantic Ocean.
2. There was an island situated in front of the straits which are by you called the Pillars of Heracles ... (Jowett) ... in front of the mouth which you Greeks call, as you say, 'the pillars of Heracles'... (Bury) There was an island opposite the strait which you call (so you say) the Pillars of Heracles ... (Lee)	The island of Atlantis was located in front of or opposite the Straits of Gibraltar (Pillars of Hercules). South America is the 'island' opposite the Strait of Gibraltar. (See Fig. B.01.)
3. The island was larger than Libya and Asia put together ...	Atlantis was a continent as large as Libya (North Africa) and Asia combined and is presently called 'South America'.
4. ... and was the way to other islands ...	Beyond South America there are islands in the Pacific ...
5. ... and from these you might pass to the whole of the opposite continent which surrounded the true ocean ...	... which lead to 'the opposite continent', that is, to Asia, the true ocean being the Atlantic and Pacific combined and which surrounds all of the Earth.
Now in this island of Atlantis there was a great and wonderful empire which had rule over the whole island and several others, and over parts of the continent, furthermore, the men of Atlantis had subjected the parts of Libya within the columns of Heracles as far as Egypt, and of Europe as far as Tyrrhenia. This vast power, gathered into one, endeavoured to subdue at a blow our country and yours and the whole of the region within the straits	This sounds like a description of the war by the 'Sea Peoples' against Egypt which took place around 1226 BC and 1186 BC. The 'Sea Peoples' also advanced by land, entering Egypt from Palestine and Libya.

6. Afterwards there occurred violent earthquakes and floods; and the island of Atlantis in like manner disappeared in the depths of the sea ... (Jowett) At a later time there occurred portentous earthquakes and floods, and one grievous day and night befell them, and the island of Atlantis in like manner was swallowed up by the sea and vanished ... (Bury) At a later time there were earthquakes and floods of extraordinary violence, and in one single dreadful day and night the island of Atlantis was swallowed up by the sea and vanished ... (Lee)	Atlantis was destroyed by earthquakes and floods. The Altiplano has periodically been subject to climatic change in the form of alternating inland seas (Lakes Minchin, Tauca, Coipasa) and dry periods. It is also prone to earthquakes, evidence of which can be seen at Pampa Aullagas where the volcano and the surrounding plain has been sunk by earthquakes. Former shorelines can be seen on the surrounding mountains and the island has a ring around it of coral-like deposits from the lake. It was only the capital island city of Atlantis which sank into the sea, not the whole continent. (See Fig. B.02)
7. For which reason the sea in those parts is impassable and impenetrable, because there is a shoal of mud in the way; and this was caused by the subsidence of the island. (Jowett) ... wherefore also the ocean at that spot has now become impassable and unsearcheable, being blocked up by the shoal mud which the island threw up as it settled down. (Bury) ... this is why the sea in that area is to this day impassable to navigation, which is hindered by mud just below the surface, the remains of the sunken island. (Lee)	The inland sea of Lake Poopó formerly called Lake Aullagas is sometimes entirely impassable to boats when it dries up in the dry season. Plato implied that the island of Atlantis was swallowed up by the sea and disappeared beneath the earth, but Sir Francis Bacon said Plato got it wrong and the sea rose to cover the city. It seems that a combination of both events took place since parts of the island have disappeared while the lake deposits show it has also been underwater.
From Critias:	**Interpretation and comments**
Nine thousand was the sum of years which had elapsed since the war.	Nine thousand years previously was given as the date for the founding of Athens but is also given as the date for the war and end of Atlantis. Clearly there is an error here, but if the nine thousand years were taken as lunar months then it would be 1260 BC which is the date of the Trojan war and more or less the date of the founding of Athens (1400 BC) by Theseus. It is unlikely that Atlantis could have existed on the Altiplano in 9600 BC since at that time the plain had already been under the waters of Lake Coipasa for some time unless it was Lake Coipasa which destroyed the city in 11,000 BC. When Lake Coipasa dried up, there were periods of alternating droughts and floods and Atlantis could have begun in any of these periods continuing perhaps up to the date of around 1260 BC (substituting months for years) which Plato gave for the war and Atlantis' subsequent destruction.

8. Looking towards the sea, but in the centre of the whole island, there was a plain ... (Jowett) Bordering on the sea and extending through the centre of the whole island there was a plain ... (Bury) At the centre of the island (i.e. midway along its greatest length,) near the sea, was a plain ... (Lee)	This plain is the Altiplano, which not only is on the centre of the whole continent but, as Lee says, it is *midway along its longest side.* (See Fig. B.03.)
9. Near the plain again, and also in the centre of the island at a distance of about fifty stadia, there was a mountain not very high on any side. (Jowett) ... and, moreover, near the plain, over against its centre, at a distance of about fifty stades, there stood a mountain that was low on all sides. (Bury) ... and near the middle of this plain about fifty stades inland a hill of no great size. (Lee)	At this location we find the volcanic mountain of Pampa Aullagas, a central cone on top of a low plateau fifty stades or five miles from the inland sea of Lake Poopó. The mountain is 'low on all sides' at Pampa Aullagas. (See Fig. B.04.)
10. Thereon dwelt one of the natives originally sprung from the earth ... and Poseidon, being smitten with desire for her, wedded her. (Bury)	This corresponds to the tale of Tunupa, God of the lakes and rivers who as Thunapa in female form married Azanaques, god of a hill opposite Pampa Aullagas.
11. Poseidon ... breaking the ground, enclosed the hill all round, making alternate zones of sea and land larger and smaller, encircling one another; so that no man could get to the island, for ships and voyages were not as yet ... (Jowett) Poseidon ... to make the hill impregnable he broke it off all round about; and he made circular belts of sea and land enclosing one another alternately, some greater, some smaller, so as to be impassable for man; for at that time neither ships nor sailing were yet in existence. (Bury) Poseidon ... fortified the hill by enclosing it with concentric rings of sea and land, making the place impassable for man (for there were still no ships or sailing in those days) ... (Lee)	In the Bolivian story, Thunapa ran away from Azanaques and laid down in Pampa Aullagas, thus creating the ringed formation there, described as *zones*, *belts* or *rings*. Pampa Aullagas has remains of these zones of land and formerly sea when the lake level was higher. (See Figs. B.05 and B.06.)

12. There were two of land and three of water, which he turned as with a lathe, each having its circumference equidistant every way from the centre ... (Jowett) ... two being of land and three of sea, which he carved as it were out of the midst of the island; and these belts were at even distances on all sides ... (Bury) There were two rings of land and three of sea, like cartwheels, with the island at their centre and equidistant from each other ... (Lee)	At Pampa Aullagas there is an outer zone of land, an inner gully or depression representing a former zone of sea, another zone of land and within that another gully depression then the central hill five stades wide. (See Fig. B.07.)
13. Beginning from the sea they bored a canal of three hundred feet in width and one hundred feet in depth and fifty stadia in length, which they carried through to the outermost zone, making a passage from the sea up to this, which became a harbour, and leaving an opening sufficient to enable the largest vessels to find ingress.	At Pampa Aullagas there is to this day a canal or river which leads from the sea to the outer ring at the site and continues on to the level plain. (See Fig. B.08.)
14. Moreover, they divided the zones of land which parted the zones of sea, leaving room for a single trireme to pass out of one zone into another. They covered over the channels so as to leave a way underneath for the ships; for the banks were raised considerably above the water.	The outer ring at Pampa Aullagas has a gap where ships could have sailed through. The rings of land are also raised just above the former level of the lake.
15. Now the largest of the zones into which a passage was cut from the sea was three stadia in breadth, and the zone of land which came next of equal breadth; but the next two zones, the one of water, the other of land, were two stadia, and the one which surrounded the central island was a stadium only in width.	The outer ring of water at Pampa Aullagas has disappeared as has the southern section of the site. A part ring of land remains with a depression on the inside where there are stones covered in deposits from the lake showing it was at one time under water. On the inside of that there is another steep ring of land and on the inside of that another gully or depression with the central island beyond that.
16. The island in which the palace was situated had a diameter of five stadia	The central island or cone at Pampa Aullagas is five stades wide.
17. The island and the circles they encompassed with a wall of stone. (Bury)	Remains of a wall of stone run round the island.
18. ... some being white, some black and some red.	Black, red and white stones are found at Pampa Aullagas.
19. Some of their buildings were simple, but in others they put together different stones, varying the colour to please the eye, and to be a natural source of delight.	At nearby Quillacas, the local church is built of red, black and white stones varied to give a pleasing appearance. (See Fig. B.09.)

20. It had mineral resources from which were mined both solid materials and metals, including one metal which survives today only in name, but was then mined in quantities in a number of locations in the island, orichalc, in those days the most valuable metal except gold. (Lee) 'a completely unknown and imaginary metal' (Lee) In the first place they dug out of the earth whatever was to be found there, mineral as well as metal, and that which is only a name and was something more than a name then, orichalc, was dug out of the earth in many parts of the island, and except gold was the most precious of metals. (Jowett) Metals to begin with, both the hard kind and the fusible kind, which are extracted by mining, and also that kind which is now known only by name but was more then a name then, there being mines of it in many parts of the island — I mean 'orichalcum' which was the most precious of the metals then known, except gold. i.e. 'mountain copper', a 'sparkling' metal hard to identify. (Bury)	Orichalcum is considered by Sir Desmond Lee to be *'a completely unknown and imaginary metal'*. But such a natural alloy exists only in the Andes where it is called *tumbaga*. It can be polished and the copper surface dissolved out to resemble pure gold.
21. The entire circuit of the wall, which went round the outermost zone, they covered with a coating of brass, and the circuit of the next wall they coated with tin, and the third, which encompassed the citadel, flashed with the red light of orichalcum. (Jowett) And they covered with brass, as though with a plaster, all the circumference of the wall which surrounded the outermost circle; and that of the inner one they coated with tin; and that which encompassed the acropolis itself with orichalcum which sparkled like fire. (Bury) And they covered the whole circuit of the outermost wall with a veneer of bronze, they fused tin over the inner wall and orichalc gleaming like fire over the wall of the acropolis itself. (Lee)	The walls were covered in brass, tin and orichalcum according to Jowett and Bury, but according to Lee the order was bronze, tin and orichalcum. Brass is an alloy of copper and zinc. Bronze is an alloy of copper and tin. Orichalcum is an alloy of gold and copper. All these metals and alloys are plentiful in the region around Lake Poopó, Bolivia including a mountain of tin next to a mountain of silver at Potosi.
22. All the outside of the temple, with the exception of the pinnacles, they covered with silver,	Nearby Potosi was a mountain of solid silver. (See Fig. B.10.)
23. ... and the pinnacles with gold	Gold was abundant in pre-Inca times.

In the interior of the temple the roof was of ivory, curiously wrought everywhere with gold and silver and orichalcum. (Jowett)	All these metals exist all around the plain and Lake Poopó.
The roof was ivory picked out with gold, silver and orichalc. (Lee) The roof was all ivory *in appearance*, variegated with gold and silver and orichalcum. (Bury)	Jowett and Lee say the roof was of ivory, but Bury says it was ivory in appearance, due to the mixing of the metals gold, silver and orichalcum.
... and all the other parts, the walls and pillars and floor, they coated with orichalcum ...	The naturally occurring alloy of gold and copper.
24. In the temple they placed statues of gold: And around the temple on the outside were placed statues of gold of all the descendants of the ten kings and of their wives ...	The custom of having golden statues of their ancestors continued into the time of the Incas. (See Fig. B.11.)
25. They had such an amount of wealth as was never before possessed by kings and potentates, and is not likely ever to be again	The nearby mountain of Potosi was the source of silver which provided the wealth of the Spanish Empire. The land is also rich in gold which motivated the Spanish to its conquest.
26. He himself, being a god, found no difficulty in making special arrangements for the centre island, bringing up two springs of water from beneath the earth, one of warm water and the other of cold.	Hot and cold springs exist on the Altiplano and can be seen at Pazna. Underground pools also exist at Pampa Aullagas. (See Fig. B.12.)
27. ... and they were wonderfully adapted for use by reason of the pleasantness and excellence of their waters.	On the Island of the Sun in Lake Titicaca can be seen Inca springs with different types of water according to their properties. (See Fig. B.13.)
28. Also they made cisterns, some open to the heavens, others roofed over, to be used in winter as warm baths ...	At Pazna on the other side of Lake Poopó can be seen thermal baths and a large stone bath open to the elements.
29. The entire area was densely crowded with habitations; and the canal and the largest of the harbours were full of vessels and merchants coming from all parts, who, from their numbers, kept up a multitudinous sound of human voices, and din and clatter of all sorts night and day.	From Pampa Aullagas, one could travel by boat to the far north-west corner of the plain or even as far away as to the northern end of Lake Titicaca, a distance of some 300 miles. The Uru culture was very much a water borne culture thriving along the aquatic axis of the Altiplano.
Because of their headship, they had a large supply of imports from abroad. (See Fig. B.14.)	It is a very large continent and 'imports from abroad' could simply mean from other parts of the continent. However, in the museum at Oruro may be seen an amphora similar to those from the Eastern Mediterranean and the Fuente Magna dish found near Lake Titicaca with cuneiform writing also suggests a contact with ancient Sumeria.

I will now describe the plain, as it was fashioned by nature and by the labours of many generations of kings through long ages.	
30. The whole country was said by him to be very lofty and precipitous on the side of the sea, but the country immediately about and surrounding the city was a level plain, itself surrounded by mountains which descended towards the sea ... (Jowett) The whole region rose sheer out of the sea to a great height, but the part about the city was all a smooth plain, enclosing it round about, and being itself encircled by mountains which stretched as far as to the sea ... (Bury) To begin with the region as a whole was said to be high above the level of the sea, from which it rose precipitously; the city was surrounded by a uniformly flat plain, which was in turn enclosed by mountains which came right down to the sea. (Lee)	Note Jowett's translation: '....*precipitous on the side of the sea*' The Altiplano is enclosed by mountains which just like the description, rise sheer out of the sea to a great height on the Western side of the continent, that is, on the side of the Pacific Ocean. The whole region, as Plato says, is high above the level of the (Ocean) sea and the mountains enclose it round about.
31. The plain was smooth and even ... (Jowett) ... and this plain had a level surface ... (Bury) ... a uniformly flat plain ... (Lee)	The Altiplano is smooth and level, the largest level plain in the world. (See Fig. B.15.)
32. ... and of an oblong shape, It was for the most part rectangular and oblong ... (Jowett) ... and was as a whole rectangular in shape, This plain was rectangular in shape, It was originally a quadrangle, rectilinear for the most part, and elongated ... (Bury) It was naturally a long, regular rectangle ... (Lee)	The Altiplano near Lake Poopó is indeed rectangular in shape and elongated, or as Lee says, a long, narrow rectangle. (See Fig. B.16.)
33. ... being 3,000 stades long on either side and 2,000 stades wide at its centre, reckoning upwards from the sea. (Bury) ... measuring three thousand stades in length and at its mid-point two thousand stades in breadth from the coast. (Lee)	The Altiplano near Lake Poopó is in the proportion of 3,000 long by 2,000 wide, the unit here being half a stade, that is, 300 ft instead of the Greek 600 ft stade. The original 300 ft stade is the length of the side of the 'Tower of Babylon'.

34. ... and what it lacked of this shape they made right by means of a trench dug round about it. Now, as regards the depth of this trench and its breadth and length, it seems incredible that it should be so large as the account states, considering that it was made by hand, and in addition to all the other operations, but nonetheless we must report what we heard: It was dug out to the depth of a plethrum and to a uniform breadth of a stade, and since it was dug round the whole plain its consequent length was 10,000 stades. (Bury) The plain was for the most part rectangular and oblong, and where falling out of the straight line followed the circular ditch. (Jowett) It (the canal) made a complete circuit of the plain, running round the city from both directions, and there discharging into the sea ... (Lee) ... and (the canal) winding round the plain ... (Donnelly 1949)	In the desert north-west of Lake Poopó there is a feature resembling a giant canal of the dimensions Plato has given. It joins pools of natural underground springs and is used by the locals to pasture their flocks. The elevations of the rectangular Altiplano are such that a canal could be dug around its perimeter in the fashion Plato described. (See Fig. B.17.) It is the plain which is rectangular and measures 3,000 x 2,000 'stades', sometimes the canal system is shown in a chequerboard pattern but other translations say it 'wound its way around the plain' implying it followed natural contours and avoided obstacles such as volcanic outcrops.
35. The depth, and width, and length of this ditch were incredible, and gave the impression that a work of such extent, in addition to so many others, could never have been artificial. Nevertheless I must say what I was told. It was excavated to the depth of a hundred, feet, and to a uniform breadth of a stade.	The section visited on site was over one stade or 600 ft wide and the archaeologists had the impression it could not have been artificial, however a local geologist studying air photos of the feature asserted it was indeed artificial.
36. It received the streams which came down from the mountains and after circling round the plain, and coming towards the city on this side and on that, it discharged them thereabouts into the sea.	There are streams which come down from the mountains surrounding the plain and a perimeter canal could discharge them into Lake Poopó.
37. And on the inland side of the city channels were cut in straight lines, of about 100 feet in width, across the plain, and these discharged themselves into the trench on the seaward side, the distance between each being 100 stades.	Parallel channels in straight lines still exist today south of Oruro on the shores of Lake Poopó and many are still in use by the people there for cultivations. (See Fig. B.18.)
38. It was in this way that they conveyed to the city the timber from the mountains and transported also on boats the seasons' products, by cutting transverse passages from one channel to the next and also to the city.	There were formerly trees around the Altiplano, much of the original vegetation was destroyed by the Spaniards and the animals they brought with them. The Uru peoples still use reed boats for transportation today. (See Fig. B.19.)

39. The surrounding mountains were celebrated for their number and size and beauty, far beyond any which still exist, having in them also many wealthy villages of country folk, and rivers, and lakes, and meadows supplying food enough for every animal, wild or tame, and much wood of various sorts, abundant for each and every kind of work.	The surrounding mountains are high volcanic peaks such as Sajama (21,464 ft), Illampu (21,067 ft), Illimani (21,005 ft). And there are indeed many villages, meadows, rivers, lakes, and so on. (See Fig. B.20.)
40. Twice in the year they gathered the fruits of the earth — in winter having the benefit of the rains of heaven, and in summer the water which the land supplied by introducing streams from the canals ...	Where raised fields have been restored near Lake Titicaca they have been able to harvest two crops per year and would have been able to sustain a vastly greater population than today. The water table was a delicately balanced system and in some periods would flow from Lake Titicaca to the south whereas at other times it could flow northwards.
41. This part of the island looked towards the south, and was sheltered from the north ...	The central island cone is of a horseshoe shape, open towards the south, being sheltered by the rim of the volcano from the north.
42. He also begat and brought up five pairs of twin male children ...	In Inca legend after the flood, one of the survivors had two sets of five sons. The Aymara kingdoms around Lake Poopó were similarly divided into twin kingdoms and, according to Huaman Poma, the first inhabitants were also born in pairs.
43. Moreover, there were a great number of elephants in the island ...	Skeletons of mastodons may be seen in the museum in Tarija and have recently been found around Lake Titicaca and to the west of Oruro.
44. There was provision for all other sorts of animals, both for those which live in lakes and marshes and rivers, and also for those which live in mountains and on plains ...	The country is full of lakes, marshes and rivers.
45. Also whatever fragrant things there now are in the earth, whether roots, or herbage, or woods, or essences which distil from fruit and flower, grew and thrived in that land ...	The area also grows every conceivable product in abundance. (See Fig. B.21.)
46. And of the inhabitants of the mountains and of the rest of the country there was also a vast multitude ...	Huaman Poma recorded that there was a vast population before the time of the Incas and that the watercourses, reservoirs and so on, could not easily be repeated.
47. Pampa Aullagas	*Pampa* means 'level plain' in Quechua, and *aullagas* also means *ullada* or *hoyada* meaning 'no more' that is, the sunken pampa.
48. The name 'Atlantis': 'Atl' means 'water' in Aztec Nahuatl language. In the wet season large parts of Amazonia are under water	*Uma* is the Aymara word for water and *Umasuyo* = the kingdom of water. The Altiplano itself was also a water kingdom with its inland seas of Lakes Titicaca and Poopó connected by the River Desaguadero.

49. The name 'Atlantis': 'Antis' means 'copper' in Quechua of the Incas. It is also the origin of the 'Andes' mountains making Atlantis the perfect name for the continent we today call South America.	The Inca name for one quarter of their empire was 'Antisuyo' — kingdom of the Antis Indians.
50. For many generations, as long as the divine nature lasted in them, they were obedient to the laws, for they possessed true and in every way great spirits, uniting gentleness with wisdom in the various chances of life, and in their intercourse with one another. They despised everything but virtue, caring little for their present state of life, and thinking lightly of the possession of gold and other property, which seemed only a burden to them: neither were they intoxicated by luxury; nor did wealth deprive them of their self-control. But they were sober, and saw clearly that all these goods are increased by virtue and friendship with one another, whereas by too great regard and respect for them, they are lost and friendship with them … But when the divine portion began to fade away, and became diluted too often and too much with the mortal admixture, and the human nature got the upper hand, they then, being unable to bear their fortune, behaved unseemly, and to him who had an eye to see grew visibly debased, for they were losing the fairest of their precious gifts; but to those who had no eye to see the true happiness, they appeared glorious and blessed at the very time when they were full of avarice and unrighteousness power. Zeus, the god of gods, who rules according to law, and is able to see into such things, perceiving that an honourable race was in a woeful plight, and wanting to inflict punishment on them, that they might be chastened and improve, collected all the gods into their most holy habitation, which, being placed in the centre of the world, beholds all created things. And when he had called them together, he spake as follows ...	According to the Bolivian legend, the god Tunupa walked amongst the people and tried to persuade them from their bad habits but was cast adrift in a boat and eventually drowned in the waters of Pampa Aullagas when the city was also destroyed by earthquakes and floods sent as a punishment by the gods. (See Fig. B.22.) Just as Poseidon was a friend to humankind and god of the Sea, Tunupa was similarly a friend to mankind, god of the lakes, rivers and inland seas. In the Greek version it is Zeus, god of the sky and hurler of thunderbolts who calls the gods together and destroys the city whereas in Bolivian legend it is Kjuni, god of wind and rain who destroys the previous inhabitants in a great flood. Other versions say it was Viracocha, the great creator god who destroyed an earlier race of giants in a great flood.

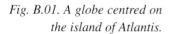

*Fig. B.01. A globe centred on
the island of Atlantis.*

*Fig. B.02. Lake Tauca
covering the Altiplano.*

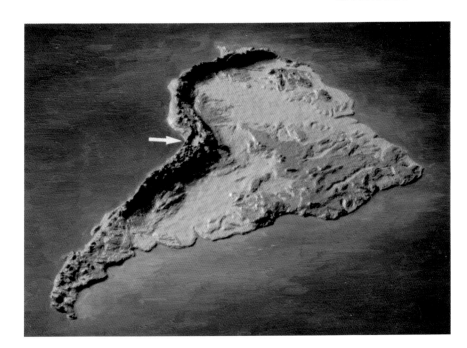

Fig. B.03. Oblique view show-ing the 'whole island' with the plain arrowed.

Fig. B.04. The mountain 'low on all sides' at Pampa Aullagas.

Fig. B.05 (above) and B.06.
Former zones of land and sea.

Fig. B.07. Former zone of sea.

Fig. B.08 (left). Channel which leads from the site at Pampa Aullagas to the sea (Lake Poopó) about 5 miles away.

Fig. B.09. Quillacas Church with stomework in black, red and white.

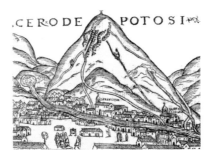

Fig. B.10. The silver mountain at Potosi was a fountain of wealth for the Spanish Empire.

Fig. B.11. Gold mask.

Fig. B.12. Hot springs.

Fig. B.13. Inca springs with three different types of water seen to the left of the stairway.

Fig. B.14. Fuente
Magna.

Fig. B.15. View of the uniformly flat plain.

Fig. B.16. The rectangular plain.

Fig. B.18. Satellite images show canals in parallel straight lines.

Fig. B.17. View looking into section of giant channel, one stade wide, to the west of Lake Poopó.

Fig. B.19. Reed boat on Lake Titicaca.

Fig. B.20. Lake Macaya.

Abundaba tanto la riqueza que no habían pobres. La vida era una continua alegría, y como no existían penas ni dolores que mitigar a todos se les había endurecido el corazón.

Fig. B.22. Legend of Tunupa.

Fig. B.21. Market in La Paz.

Appendix C: Greek Gods

Cronos

Principal figure in Greek mythology

From Chronos and Rhea ...

Zeus

Overthrew his father, Cronos.

Battle between Zeus and his brothers and sisters known as Titans and other beings continued until Zeus defeated Typhon. Zeus becomes Father of Gods and Men, Master of the celestial fire. His chief weapon is the thunderbolt.

A king upon Earth who had descended from the Heavens. Known as God of the skies.

Hades

Unseen, aloof, forbidding, stern. Known as God of the Underworld. Territory encompassed marshlands, desolate areas, land watered by mighty rivers.

Synonym for hell.

... Poseidon

Master of metallurgy, sculpting, magician, friend to humankind, known as God of the Sea, his symbol is the trident.

Displeased by the greed and behaviour of its inhabitants, destroys the island and city of Atlantis in earthquakes and floods.

Inherited island of Atlantis and married a woman who lived on a hill next to the sea and in the centre of a rectangular level plain. Created circular defensive formation around it.

Has five pairs of twin sons to rule the island of Atlantis.

Appendix D: Andean Gods

Kon-Tiki, or Viracocha in Quechua, ruler of the universe, friend and teacher of mankind.

Pachacamac, creator of the Universe, 'earth maker' originally from Yungas — also known as

Tunupa in Aymara sometimes considered to be a son of Viracocha or another version of Viracocha, a teacher of humankind.

God of storms and of the sun. Destroys an early race in a great flood. Creates the sun and moon.

One survivor has two wives and ten sons in two lineages each of five sons.

Viracocha wanders throughout the country bringing civilization to the inhabitants before disappearing over the Pacific Ocean.

Inti the Sun god, son of Viracocha, consort is **Mama Quilla,** moon goddess, earth mother and fertility goddess.

Tunupa, was god of lakes, rivers and inland seas.

Cast adrift in a balsa boat in Lake Titicaca, opens up the Desaguadero River and disappears under the waters of Pampa.

In Inca mythology, **Manco Capac,** the first Inca, is the son of Inti, his wife and sister is **Mama Ocllo**, daughter of Inti.

Re-emerges in female form as **Thunapa**, married a person who lived on a hill in the centre of the rectangular plain and created rings of land around it.

In Inca creation myth, **Manco Capac** is also descended from Viracocha, one of 'four pairs of brother-sisters created by Viracocha to rule the world.' The 'world' being the Inca world of Tahuantinsuyo — that is, South America, or formerly 'Atlantis'.

Kon, God of wind and rain, son of Inti, and Mama Quilla also known as **Kjuni,** destroyed giants in a great flood before humankind existed and destroyed a great city on a lake by floods and storms.

Pachamama, Provider of food and pastures sometimes said to be earth mother and fertility goddess.

Mama Cocha said to be sea goddess and wife of Viracocha.

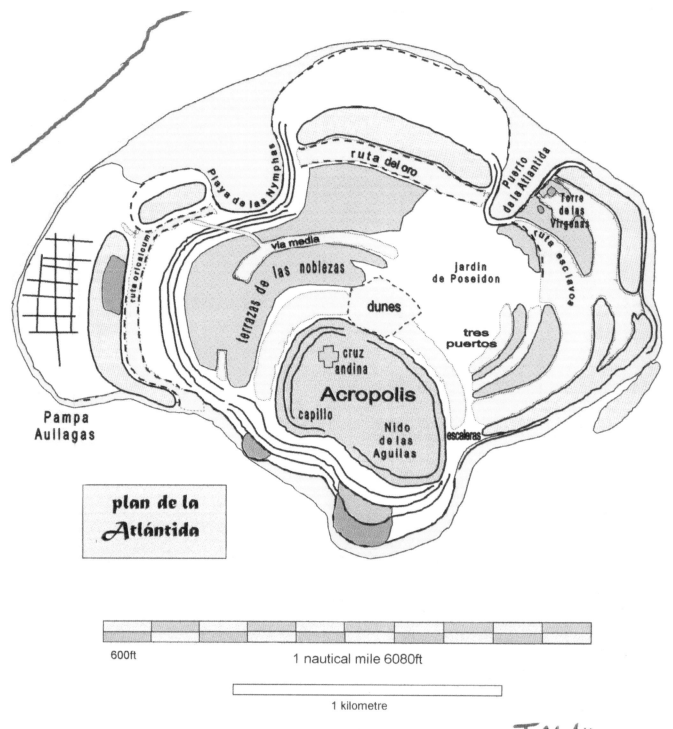

Tourist Map of Atlantis at Pampa Aullagas.

References and Sources

Allen, J.M. (1998) *Atlantis: the Andes Solution*, Windrush Press, UK.

—, (2001) *La Ruta de la Atlántida,* Latinas Editores, Oruro, Bolivia.

Aveni, Anthony F. (2000) *Empires of Time*, I.B. Taurus & Co., London and New York.

Bacon, Francis (1627) *The New Atlantis*, modern edition (1900) Cambridge University Press.

Baker, Paul A., Dunbar, Robert B. *et al.* (2001) 'The history of South American tropical climate for the past 25,000 years from the sedimentary record of Lake Titicaca (Bolivia/Peru)', *Science,* Vol.291, 5504, January 26, 2001, pp. 640–43.

Berossus (3rd cent bc) in Isaac Preston Cory (ed.), *Ancient Fragments*, William Pickering, London, 1832.

Bellamy, H.S. (1947) *Built before the Flood*, Faber and Faber, UK.

Blashford-Snell, John (2008) 'An Amazonian Adventure, Phase VII', Scientific Exploration Society, in *Past Horizons* online journal, Issue 4, Sep. 2008.

Blavatsky, H.P. (1877) *Isis Unveiled*, Theosophical Publishing House, NY.

Braghine, Col. A. (1940/1980) *The Shadow of Atlantis*, The Aquarian Press Ltd.

Brown, Dale (1994) *The Search for El Dorado*, Time-Life Books.

Bruhns, Karen Olsen (1994) *Ancient South America,* Cambridge University Press.

Bury, R. G., (1929) Plato IX *Timaeus, Critias, Cleitophon, Menexenus, Epistles*, Harvard University Press, Cambridge, Mass., US.

Candia, Don Antonio Paredes (1998) *Leyendas de Bolivia*, La Paz, Bolivia.

Corvison, Oscar (1996) *Calendario Solar Vigésimal de Tiwanaku*, La Paz.

Coote, Stephen (1993) *A Play of Passion, the life of Sir Walter Ralegh,* Macmillan, London.

Donnelly, Ignatius (1949) rep. of 1882 edition, Sampson, Low, Marston & Co., London and Edinburgh.

Gamboa, Pedro Sarmiento de (1572) *Historia de los Incas*, Peru (see Markham 1907).

Graves, Robert (1955) *The Greek Myths,* Penguin, UK.

Gómara, Franciso López de (1552) *La Historia de las Indias*, Zaragoza.

Kendall, Ann (1973) *Everyday Life of the Incas,* B.T. Batsford, London.

Klein, Herbert S. (1992) *Bolivia,* Oxford University Press, USA.

Lee, Desmond (1965) Plato *Timaeus* and *Critias*, Penguin Books, UK.

Markham, Sir Clements (1907) *History of the Incas*, (translation of Pedro Sarmiento de Gamboa, 1572, above), The Hakluyt Society, Cambridge University Press, UK.

Maspero, G. (nd.) *History of Egypt, Chaldea, Syria, Babylonia and Assyria*, trans. M.L. McClure, The Grolier Society, London.

Montaño, Mario (1979) *Raíces Semíticas en la Religiosidad Aymara y Kichua,* La Paz, Bolivia.

Ondegardo, Polo de (1571) *Los errores y supersticiones de los Indios,* Peru.

Posnansky, Arthur (1937) *Antropología y sociología andina*, La Paz.

—, (1945) *Tihuanacu, the Cradle of American Man,* J.J. Augustin, NY.

Redfield James (1997) *The Celestine Prophecy,* Warner Books, USA.

Rohl, David (1999) *Legend — the Genesis of Civilization,* Arrow Books, UK.

Thom, A. (1967) *Megalithic Sites in Britain,* Clarendon Press, UK.

Tompkins, Peter (1978) *Secrets of the Great Pyramid,* Penguin, UK.

Salcamaygua, Juan de Santa Cruz Pachacuti Yanqui (1603) *Crónica relación de antigüedades de este reino del Perú* (private collection), republished by Editorial Fondo de Cultura Económica, Lima, 1995.

Vega, Garcilaso de la (1609) *Comentarios reales de los Incas*, Lisbon.

Verrill, Hyatt & Ruth (1953) *America's Ancient Civilizations,* G.P. Putnam's Sons, NY.

Wilkins, Harold (1974) *Mysteries of Ancient South America,* Lyle Stuart, USA.

Background sources

For recent events (p. 38) overturning previous conceptions about the ancient history of South America, see: http://www.iht.com/articles/reuters/2008/02/25/america/OUKWD-UK-PERU-ARCHEOLOGY.php.

For background on ancient urban settlements, see: http://news.nationalgeographic.com/news/2008/08/080828-amazon-cities.html]

For discovery of a fossilized human footprint on the shores of Lake Titicaca thought to date back five to fifteen million years, see in Spanish: www.taringa.net/posts/1266261.
In English: www.javno.com/en/lifestyle/clanak.php?id=152390.

For traces of coca and tobacco (p.40) in the remains of Egyptian mummies, see: http://www.faculty.ucr.edu/~legneref/botany/mummy.htm.

For background on Viracocha (p. 65), see:
http://www.nflc.org/reach/7ca/enCAInca.htm — *Precolumbian Cultures: Andean Quechua Culture,* 'The Inca'. National Foreign Language Center, University of Maryland.

For background on Fuente Magna (p. 75) see:
http://www.world-mysteries.com/sar_8.htm.

For background on Akakor expedition (p. 77), see: http://www.akakor.com/english/tiwabrief-uk.html]

For Posnansky's (1945) figures for Tiwanaku (p. 152) see: www.parametriczone.com/zone/archive/arthur_posnansky/arthur_posnansky_5.php